35 - Smith - one man
50 - Imperialism
65-6 - Imperialism
67 - movement back to the people
       opportunism v socialism
74 Naturalist thought
112 Mill... & early capitalism
185 trends in future
116 absolutes

ECONOMIC IDEAS

A Study of Historical Perspectives

PRENTICE-HALL ECONOMICS SERIES

E. A. J. Johnson, Editor

ECONOMIC IDEAS

A Study of Historical Perspectives

by Ferdinand Zweig

Department of Economic and Social Studies, the University of Manchester
Onetime Professor of Political Economy, the University of Cracow

New York · PRENTICE-HALL, INC. · *1950*

CONTENTS

I

MEN AND IDEAS

―――――――――――

Interpreting the History

The history of economic thought, like all other history, needs to be rewritten for every generation—not only because another chapter which has enriched our experience needs to be added to its books, but because the remainder needs to be interpreted anew. Without interpretation history is meaningless. Interpretation means adding spirit and life to the mere collection of facts, taking part in the issues of the period by understanding them and not merely passing sentence on them from the judge's seat. Every generation has a deep insight into some epochs and a looser and more detached understanding of others. Every generation is interested in different parts of the immense and infinite wealth of material presented by historical experience and will therefore choose different criteria for the selection of material.

The present generation is interested above all else in the rich material presented by the mercantilist epoch. We understand better its spirit, its issues, its working ideas, its institutions. That epoch practiced the economics of control which is one of the main subjects of our own studies at the present time. Our planners today may be regarded as the grandchildren of that eventful period. Our

I

interpretation of mercantilism has long departed from that of the liberal epoch, which regarded the mercantilist writers as obscurantists, denied the true light of economic wisdom. We have much to learn from the mistakes and trials of that period, from the working of its institutions, from the limitations implied in any control.

For the same reason the canonist school of the Middle Ages with its ideas of *iustum pretium* (just price) and *iustum salarium* (just wages) presents much greater interest than in former times. We have come to realize that the idea of *iustum salarium* not only is a norm of ethical judgment, but represents a short formula of a specific behavior which influences the real process of price formation more than we supposed. The inquiry made in 1939 by the Oxford group of economists revealed that the entrepreneur in fact behaves according to his idea of a "just price." He does not act as the economic theorist of the marginal utility school depicted him as acting—trying to get the maximum value for the minimum supply—but makes a calculation of his total costs, seeking what he regards as a just bargain. It may be that six or seven centuries of Christian teaching have done more even in economics than we imagined at first, inculcating in man a certain pattern of price behavior. We grant that this price behavior was much more prevalent in the Middle Ages than now, but it still survives, and as a matter of fact is being revived and strengthened in the practice of large-scale corporations much beyond anything experienced in the nineteenth century.

There is also great interest on the part of the modern economist in the history of the socialist school, which was once treated as belonging to the field of political and social study but outside the temple of pure and objective economic analysis. We now view the so-called objectivity with different eyes, and I will have a word or two more to say about it later on.

We know that every theoretical truth is related to a certain set of assumptions, and the socialist school, consciously or unconsciously, has selected a different set of assumptions from those of the classical school. Whereas the latter saw national economic activity achieved through the operations of the individual striving for wealth and maximum profit, the socialist school selected for consideration the national interest, i.e., the interest of a nation regarded as a whole, the striving for a maximum national income.

This assumption makes many socialist tracts very interesting reading at the present time, when attention is being paid to the criterion of maximum real national income. The further contribution of the Marxist school to the understanding of a monopolistic economy is related to its assumption of the class struggle. For individuals striving for individual wealth, the Marxist school has substituted social classes striving for the maximum wealth of their members, thus throwing additional light on the economic struggle under monopolistic conditions.

The chief interest of the present-day economist is turned to the institutionalist and historical school, which stresses the importance of institutionalist setting and mass behavior for the study of economics. The modern planner is primarily an institutionalist and behaviorist.

On the other hand the marginal utility and the mathematical schools, which began with Jevons, Menger, and Walras in the seventies of the last century, have lost much of their former interest for the economist and have even come to seem antiquated, since they are based on assumptions which have lost much of their validity for our own age.

* * *

There are two kinds of approach to economic thought. One of these may be termed the historical, the other the theoretical. The historian regards economic thought as generalization on economic conditions and economic policy valid for a given age; the theorist

3

regards it as truth valid for all ages, although truth itself is hypothetical, i.e., based on a certain set of assumptions. Here at this point there is a meeting-place for the historian and the theorist. If a theoretical truth is valid for a set of assumptions, it is valid for an age for which those assumptions are correct. Every age selects its own assumptions which have the value of reality, i.e., which coincide with reality in the highest degree.

The canonist school of the Middle Ages consciously or unconsciously chose the assumption that men work to maintain their traditional standard of living but not to accumulate indefinite riches, and they thus reached the conceptions of *iustum pretium* and *iustum salarium*.

The mercantilist writers in the sixteenth and seventeenth centuries assumed that states, that is, kings and princes, are engaged in a never-ending struggle for power and wealth, and arrived at the conception of a one-sided balance of trade of an aggressive type. The classical school assumed that men as individuals are engaged in the struggle for maximum profits under highly competitive conditions, and arrived at the conception of the division of labor and of what is called *laissez-faire* economics.

These respective assumptions were related to a given age, and had the greatest practical value for their generations. People were interested in exploring the avenues opened by these assumptions because they presented the best clue for the understanding of their world. This interest is the decisive factor in developing certain fields of study, as we have to acknowledge in all disciplines and sciences. First the writer must be interested in the study, then the publisher, then the reader and the body of scholars and scientists who call the tune in any given period. It is a fair guess that all these classes will be more interested in studies conducted on realistic assumptions than in others.

When once I explained that economic theory is a hypothetical science based on a given set of assumptions, I was asked by a listener: "Well, there must be thousands, if not millions, of combinations of assumptions, and is there any chance that economic theory will progress beyond the limits of first approximations? There must be an infinite and impenetrable jungle of cases and sub-cases, and the whole science must be very casuistical with very few general principles." This seemed to me to be a very good point.

As a matter of fact the present state of economic study resembles a jungle with an infinite number of cases and sub-cases. Everyone takes up a case of his own, analyzing his own assumptions at will, starting his article or study with some such preface as: "We write for saving S, for investment I, for rate of interest R, and assume that . . . Thus we have the following sets of equations." And these are afterwards analyzed and commented on in a scholarly and mathematical way.

My answer to my listener's question was: "Our purpose is to make only assumptions that are realistic and valid, and not any odd assumptions taken from the air; this amounts to the proposition that we have to study history, past and present, and trends pointing to the future. We have to concentrate on the most interesting assumptions, because economy must be practiced in economic studies themselves. Our life, our effort, our means are all restricted, we have little time, and we must concentrate on what seems to us to be most important. And in every generation there is fortunately a large measure of agreement among economists as to which assumptions are most interesting and what problems are most pressing. The theorems based on these solid assumptions, although hypothetical in nature, are regarded by this generation as real absolute truth, just as the so-called 'pure theory' of the marginal school was so regarded twenty or thirty years ago. From these hypothetical truths generalizations are made, which penetrate deep into the consciousness of a given generation and are regarded later on by the historian of the future as its living ideas.

"When the age passes and the assumptions become hollow and empty, the generalizations resemble a deserted palace, visited by tourists and students of history and culture. The palace may be either already fallen into decay or kept in good repair. But we can always learn from its structure, architecture, and internal arrangement.

"As a matter of fact we can learn from the economic thought of past generations much more than we can learn from old palaces and houses. The truths revealed in the great ideas of the past are eternal in the sense that they are valid for all ages as long as the assumptions on which they are based continue to operate. The thought of past ages, as much as present economic theory, is eternal, and transitional at the same time, so long as it is consistent, well-developed and logical. It is eternal because it is eternally valid in relation to a given set of assumptions; it is transitional because the set of assumptions to which it is related is unlikely to be repeated in the same combination. But sometimes it might come back in its essentials, and it then assumes the importance of the reality.

"The historical thought of past generations resembles an experiment, if, of course, we take into account all the differences between an experience of history and an experiment in the laboratory."

Who Are the Economists?

The history of economic thought is concerned mainly with successful writers, although the success need not necessarily be attained during their lifetime. Success is measured by the amount of influence, primarily on contemporaries, but also on future generations. Has the writer influenced the legislation and the economic policy of his age, allowing, of course, for a longer or shorter time-lag? Has he taken an active part in molding the economic climate of his own or a subsequent generation? Has he contributed to or orginated social-economic movements? Finally, has he inspired other writers, who have drawn upon his ideas, conceptions, or school of thought? The answer to these questions will mark the dividing line between the successful and the unsuccessful writers.

In other words the dividing line is the fertility of the writers' conceptions in the realm of policy, legislation, movements, or in the realm of thought. The economic historian will concentrate first on the writers who took part in shaping reality; the historian of economic thought on those who took part in shaping the pattern of subsequent economic thought. Usually the writers who shaped the reality are at the same time the writers who shaped thought. Adam Smith, Ricardo, John Stuart Mill, Karl Marx belong to both the first and the second category. On the other hand there are a number of great writers highly fertile in the domain of thought who have little relevance to economic policy, legislation, or movement, writers such as Jevons, Menger, Walras, Wieser, or Böhm-Bawerk.

I consider the writers of the former category greater than those of the latter, because their heritage is richer and more lasting. They are also accorded No. 1 priority in the history of economic thought.

What of the unsuccessful writers rehabilitated by historians for their intellectual value? Take for instance Richard Cantillon, the distinguished author of the *Essai sur la nature du commerce en général* (1755), a book of great theoretical value, original, very progressive for his age, who expressed before Adam Smith the same ideas to be found in *The Wealth of Nations* with great, in many respects superior, consistency and purity. Jevons considered that Cantillon was the true founder of political economy. But Cantillon's work was unsuccessful, it remained obscure, although it gave birth to much of what was written by the physiocrats, by Adam Smith, and by Malthus. Quesnay, Mirabeau, Turgot, and Adam Smith were close students of Cantillon's excellent book. But it was obscured by the fame of Adam Smith, and was soon forgotten. As a result Cantillon is very lucky if he gets a line or two mentioning his name in the history of economic thought, although even the present-day reader can find in his work much of interest.

Or take Hermann Heinrich Gossen, the great forerunner of the marginal and mathematical school, who published in 1854 *Entwickelung der Gesetze des menschlichen Verkehrs*. He regarded himself as the Copernicus of modern economics, and many mathematical economists still uphold his claim. But he was unsuccessful. He sold four or five copies of his book and then, discouraged, withdrew it from circulation. He was later rediscovered by Professor Adamson of Manchester, and the discovery was made public by Jevons in the preface to the second edition of his *The Theory of Political Economy* (1879), in which he frankly stated that Gossen "had completely anticipated him as regards the general principles and methods of economics."

But Gossen had little influence on the development of economic thought, while Jevons, a less original thinker, who published his work nearly seven years later, became an important figure in the domain of economic ideas. It is therefore the success and not the originality of thought that counts in according the priority to Jevons over Gossen.

Contrast Karl Rodbertus and Karl Marx. Rodbertus, author of *Die Forderungen der arbeitenden Klasse* (1837) and of *Soziale Briefe an von Kirchman* (1850) is a highly original and profound thinker, very logical, consistent, clear and vigorous, who formu-

8

lated long before Marx the main theses of "scientific socialism," especially the "law of surplus value," the "iron law of wages," and the inevitability of the socialist transformation of society. Adolf Wagner was right in seeking to bring Rodbertus' name into prominence, even going so far as to call him the real father of socialist theory. But Rodbertus was detached from the socialist movement, which in spite of Lassalle's invitation he refused to join, and he exercised very little influence on the movements or the legislation of his time. His greatest influence was upon Lassalle himself, who borrowed from him some of his most potent ideas. Marx knew his works, but there is little possibility of proving in what degree he drew on them. But whatever the judgment, we pass on the works of Marx and Rodbertus in regard to logical and theoretical criteria; Marx stands out as a giant compared with Rodbertus because of his enormous historical significance. Marx has shaped the reality and thought of the last hundred years perhaps more than anyone else, and whoever on theoretical or logical grounds refuses to study him deprives himself of the ability to understand some of the most potent movements and transformations of modern history. There is no such thing as Rodbertusism, but Marxism certainly exists.

Similarly one may contrast Edgeworth and Marshall. Francis Edgeworth, the author of *Mathematical Physics* (1881) and many other original contributions collected in *Papers Relating to Political Economy* (3 vols.), published by the Royal Economic Society in 1925, was a very original, profound thinker with great powers of analysis and logic, while Marshall was an eclectic teacher who combined Schmoller with Jevons, the historical and institutional conception with the idea of marginal utility. Marshall himself expressed this position in the preface to the first edition of his *Principles of Economics* (1890). The substance of his work was affected by Spencer and the ethico-historical studies of the German

9

historical school, the form by the mathematical conceptions of continuity as represented in Cournot's *Principes Mathématiques de la théorie des richesses*.[1] Marshall was the best representative of the English compromise between the historical and the theoretical approaches, and his work was crowned with great success. He was the teacher of one or two generations of British and American economists, and his textbook is still read today with great interest and profit, while Edgeworth's papers were left from the beginning on the dusty shelves of libraries. Thus the economic historian devotes to Marshall's work a chapter by itself, while dismissing Edgeworth with a word or two.

Of the work of contemporaries John Maynard Keynes's great volume, *The General Theory of Employment, Interest, and Money* (1936), will survive in the history of economic thought. Keynes is the creator and architect of the doctrine of full employment accepted in nearly all English-speaking communities, the doctrine of expenditure. The White Paper on Employment (1944), the Australian White Paper, and the American recovery plans of the thirties are all based on the Keynesian conception that to ensure full employment one must maintain an adequate level of expenditure on consumption and investment combined. On the European continent the doctrine of Keynes never took hold, because the continental experience, with its succession of monetary and credit upheavals, differing monetary behavior, and lack of productive equipment, cannot rely merely on expenditure. Had Keynes been born on the Continent, and had he written for the French people, for instance, he would have remained in the background and could not have assumed his leading position as the principal economic thinker of the interwar period. The background of Keynesian economics is the interwar economy of Britain and the United States, with high propensity to save and small

---

[1] Paris 1838.

incentives to invest, with the "vanishing investment opportunities" determined by many historical factors in this period.

Without such a background, Keynes's philosophy and economics could never have exerted so powerful an influence as they have done on our generation. His greatness consists just in this: that he expressed the need of his time, and presented us with a valuable technique and weapon for dealing with the problem of unemployment. This accounts for the enormous fertility of his thought, manifest in the flood of reviews, notes, and studies devoted to or based on Keynes.

The other great source of Keynes's popularity was that the public was quick to realize the political and social value of his doctrine as the only answer and alternative to that of Marx. Keynes contended that the weakness and disorder of capitalism is only quantitative, not qualitative; that whereas it fails to produce full employment, it does not misdirect or misuse the national resources. And this weakness can be remedied by partial planning confined and limited to one segment of national economy, that of investment. Partial planning was his answer to the program of total planning developed by Marxists and other planners.

"Social Freudism"

Students of the materialist conception of history have overlooked the most important fact regarding its origin, namely, that it originated in the criticism of the economic doctrine contained in Marx's tract *Zur Kritik der politischen Oekonomie* (1859). Marx here contends that the political economy whose theories he violently criticizes is a bourgeois or class doctrine, i.e., it is based on class interests or class prejudice. Nassau Senior, who in Marx's times was the most influential economist in England, was in the forefront of the onslaught against new social legislation, especially against the attempts to shorten hours of work. Senior had argued (although he later revised his views) that the shortening of working hours would be a most deadly weapon against British industry, because the profit of the entrepreneur is made during the last hours employment of the workers, who in the remaining hours are working for themselves. The careful study of the whole controversy over social legislation in England contained in a multitude of White Papers, evidence and contra-evidence, especially the arguments of Senior, probably gave Marx the idea of relative and absolute surplus value. Marx's idea that the struggle for a standard of working time was the most important part of the struggle of the two classes was probably a generalization of the conditions prevailing in the middle of the nineteenth century.

Attacking the political economy of his time, Marx labeled it a rationalization of the interests of the ruling class, and then generalized this contention into a statement that ideas, conceptions, art, literature, law, religion are a superstructure built on the basis of productive forces. His materialistic conception of history first started in his polemic against the Utopians and against those economists whose ideology he regarded with suspicion and whose arguments he considered a façade covering something else. They could not be so foolish as to believe all that, he averred; if they had open eyes and ears and were willing to use them, they could see and hear the real truth.

Marx first applied to public and scientific consciousness what Freud later applied to individual consciousness. What a man thinks about himself is often as wrong as what a whole nation thinks about itself. Marx contended, not that the bourgeois economist is a hypocrite or a humbug, but that the real sources of his ideology, as a rule not realized even by himself, lie deeper down, in unconscious beliefs and myths related to the interests of his class. Marx's "Social Freudism" therefore existed before Freud, just as Malthus'

Darwinism existed before Darwin. Marx said: "Ideology is a process accomplished by the so-called thinker consciously, indeed, but with a false consciousness. The real motives impelling him remain unknown to him, otherwise it would not be an ideological process at all. Hence he imagines false or apparent motives."[2]

The materialist or economic conception of history, which reduces ideological categories to economic structure, has nowhere greater application than in the realm of economic thought from which Marx started. It is doubtful whether we can relate religious or artistic ideas to an economic basis with any great measure of success, but certainly economic ideas are the direct offshoot of economic conditions, economic policy, and economic interests. They are generalizations about economic conditions, justifications of an existing policy or postulations of a new economic policy, rationalizations of various economic interests.

Marx was thoroughly conversant with the history of economic thought, beginning with the Greek philosophers, Roman jurists, and the canonist theologians; and it must have struck him, as it strikes the present-day reader of the history of economic thought, that the statements of many great minds about economic conditions and relations are out of proportion to their powers of observation and reasoning. How could Aristotle contend that the institution of slavery is a necessary one, simply because a household economy needs living tools? Distinguishing between "natural" and "unnatural" modes of acquiring wealth, Aristotle regarded the hunting of either wild animals for their flesh and skins or slaves for their services as a "natural" mode. In his ideal *Republic* Plato condoned slavery as consistent with the natural and ideal order. Similarly Cato the virtuous gave advice on how to exploit

---

[2] *Letter to Mehring, 14th July 1893, Marx-Engels Correspondence.* London: Martin Lawrence, Ltd., 1934, p. 511.

slaves with the utmost rigor and severity, recommending their employment even on public holidays, thus transgressing even the commands of religion. Varro classed slaves as vocal implements among mute and semivocal tools (cattle). And the great Dominican, St. Thomas Aquinas, the Angelic Doctor of the Schools, argued that slaves are a necessity, not only because "man needs slaves," but because slavery is a consequence of Adam's fall.

The great powers of observation and reasoning of those writers, the high principles of their ethics, and the wide perspectives of their philosophy could not save them from the mistake of generalizing about existing conditions and institutions and taking sides with the interests of the ruling class. They were bound up with contemporary institutions and could imagine nothing else.

The student of the history of economic doctrines is often perplexed at finding how much bias and prejudice there is in the work of even the most enlightened, the deepest and most powerful thinkers. When the physiocrats glorify the divine right of the ownership of land, when Malthus accepts poverty as a stimulus to the production of wealth and regards it as a natural phenomenon not to be cured, when John Stuart Mill in his first period (before coming under the influence of Saint-Simon) defends his theory of the "wages fund" which served for many years as the best weapon against workers' claims for higher wages, when Senior enters with great passion upon the fight against shortening hours of work, when Jevons discourages and abuses trade-unionism, we realize that even the greatest minds are not wholly free from the blight of bias and prejudice. Marx said that their prejudice is to a great extent class prejudice, being mostly a rationalization of the existing interests and institutions.

We may therefore say that in a certain epoch within a certain social group the basic beliefs and dogmas which serve as more or less unconscious assumptions of individual doctrines are strikingly alike, and they are linked with the basic institutions of a given period. The details of doctrine are individual and personal, but the structure is collective and historical. A psychologist would say that the substance and content of consciousness is individual and detailed, expressed in individual lines of thought, but that the subconsciousness is collective, based on the experience of the whole group, grounded in the past and present conditions, and expressed in the climate of a thought or culture pattern.

In fact every doctrine has not only its conscious part, its superstructure visible to everybody, but also its "subconscious" part hidden behind the surface, its soul and spirit, which need searching and penetrating. Has not, for instance, the marginal utility school a depth of assumption, half consciously or subconsciously made, rooted in the whole philosophy of life and the atmosphere of the second half of the nineteenth century? What is called "Tiefen psychology" (the psychology of depths) has full application to economic and social doctrines, and the collective social subconsciousness hides many treasures for any investigator willing to explore it.

When Aristotle spoke about the "necessity" of the institution of slavery, he was probably not aware of the basic assumptions which subconsciously lay behind this conception; in the same way many modern economic writers are often unaware of those great forces and currents operating in the back of their minds. And here is the explanation why many ideas which look erroneous when the superstructure only is envisaged look different when the collective subconsciousness is taken into account. The comparison of the two layers of our mind to an iceberg floating in the ocean with one-eighth of its bulk visible above the water and seven-eighths below holds good also for the analysis of our social-economic doctrines. The great interest shown in the marginal utility school, the great enthusiasm with which it was greeted in nearly all centers of learning, was, I believe, not for the one-eighth visible above the water but for the seven-eighths below. How many times has the exposition of the marginal utility school turned by its very nature into glorification of the laissez-faire system with all that it implied?

Thus it is that doctrines have their secrets as much as individuals have theirs, and close scrutiny would substantially promote our understanding of economic teaching and give a new insight into the foundations of social and economic ideas.

Are the Greatest Minds Attracted to the Study of Economics?

Is it the greatest minds, or only inferior or average ones, that are attracted to economic studies? Alfred Marshall asked this question, and was not very sure of the answer. Many a historian of economic thought has wondered why the Greek scholars had so little to say about the economic life of their time, which was quite complex and in process of great changes. Why did the Roman writers, who showed such great powers of abstraction and analysis in legal matters, have no comment to make on the problems of international economy of their time, highly developed as it was with complex and specialized institutions? The argument already stated by McCulloch was that the subject of the pursuit of wealth seemed unworthy of the philosopher's quest, since labor, the basis of all wealth, was looked upon as degrading. But even in Christian times, when labor assumed the dignity of prayer, we do not find great minds attracted to the study of wealth. Marshall admitted that he himself was at first repelled by the idea that the making of wealth could be worthy of scientific study: "Indeed," he said, "a science which has wealth for its subject matter is often repugnant at first sight to many students; for those who do most to advance the boundaries of knowledge, seldom care much about the possession of wealth for its own sake."

The fact remains that the greatest minds, who have made the largest contribution to the treasury of economic thought, regarded economics only as a side issue among their interests and took up its study relatively late in their lives, after devoting much of their effort to other subjects. Aristotle and Thomas Aquinas dealt only incidentally with economic questions. Bodin, Locke, Hume, Bentham were not economists, although they made contributions to economic study. Nicole Oresme, the author of *De origine, jure, et mutationibus monetarum* (c. 1356–1361) was Bishop of Lisieux; Nicolas Copernicus, author of the important tract *Monete cudende ratio* (1526) written for King Sigismund I of Poland, was an astronomer. François Quesnay, the founder of the physiocratic doctrine, was physician to Madame de Pompadour and author of the *Essai physique sur l'économie animale* (1736). He first took an interest in economics when about 56 or 57 years old, and his first economic essays, *Fermiers* and *Grains,* were published under a pseudonym. Adam Smith was a moral philosopher and a historian, Malthus a moral philosopher and student of population, John Stuart Mill a logician and philosopher, David Ricardo a retired, wealthy stockbroker; Thornton, Tooke, Newmarch were successful business men and bank directors; Sismondi was a historian, Le Play a social reformer.

It would never have occurred to Karl Marx to call himself an economist. Pareto was an engineer, Rodbertus a landlord and farmer. Roscher, Schmoller, Wagner, Brentano, Knies, Bücher, Max Weber were primarily historians and sociologists. Frederick List was a man of affairs, journalist, and politician. Even Alfred Marshall proves the rule, for his studies started with other interests, mathematics, ethics, and philosophy, and he very soon dropped his

interest in economics, writing very little after his first volume, the
Principles of Economics in 1890.

What of Lord Keynes? Very little has been published so far on
the life of Keynes, but when the biographies of him do appear, they
will show that he also proves the rule. Keynes was a very active
man of affairs, attracted first to philosophy and mathematics,
writing on the calculus of probability. Economics hardly formed
the main center of his life interests.

If great minds do not take enough interest in economics to de-
vote their whole life to its study, it is not only because they regard
the mere pursuit of wealth as an unworthy object of their interests,
but also, perhaps, because they expect very little scholarly reward
for their studies. Economic phenomena are so changeable and
varying that to grasp them is like holding drops of water in one's
hand. They slip through. To generalize over them is certainly to
head for failure. On the other hand, to reason in the abstract on
the basis of a few assumptions is to play a game of little profit and
less use in real life. The great minds are discouraged, seeing the
multitude of doctrines, schools, and systems of economics contending with each other and making little progress because they lack
the stable foundations on which to build a progressively expanding
home.

The fact remains that the great stimuli to economic thought
came from outside, whether from new legal conceptions; or from
medicine, physics, mathematics, statistics, psychology, technology,
sociology; or from great social reform movements. The enrich-
ment of economic thought has rarely come from the rank and file
of professional economists. The so-called professional economist
has mainly been a bore, a more or less barren bore, who could carry
on for a time the work entrusted to him by the great outsiders, but
very soon realized that the soil, unenriched by new fertilizing
material, becomes exhausted and sterile.

The Principle of Selection

The principle of selection is the most powerful and most useful tool of the historian and at the same time his greatest drawback. The historian presents a picture, not a photograph, of a period. In that respect he resembles a painter, who also has to select. His selection is based on his interpretation, and here there comes into play not only all his theory and knowledge, but also his bias and prejudice. Since he has to select, he must throw overboard much that may be valuable, and even essential. The historian must know what is essential, but the conception of the essential in itself involves an appreciation and very often a value judgment. From this it follows that all historiography is deeply rooted in our orientation, i.e., in our values and theories, which change with time. It follows also that very often when we think that history teaches us a theory or a moral, it is only because that theory or that moral was prior to the historical description, and guided our hand in the drawing of the picture.

A more important drawback is that the more selective historiography is, the less is it historically true. Everyone knows that a highly selective historiography amounts to a theory, and some of these selective pictures are very fashionable among economic historians as for instance that of mercantilism, covering the entire period between the Middle Ages and the age of *laissez-faire,* or the highly selective picture of capitalism, or that of the Industrial Revolution.

Actually neither mercantilism nor capitalism existed in the sense in which a factory or an industry exists. Each concept was a product of imagination and selection. We grasp the characteristics of a given period or movement in the belief that they are essential. We form what Max Weber called an "Ideal type," which is the product not merely of abstraction but of the addition of certain features and the diminution of others which together form a consistent or rather a convincing picture.

A historian has to choose between forming highly selective pictures and merely recording facts. In the former case he is more theoretical, in the second more "historical." This means that a true historian likes to write exhaustive and voluminous works on even the smallest and shortest sectors of historical experience, because in such works he can do more justice to the wealth of material. In contrast a short work which covers a huge period must be highly selective, and must therefore give only a rough and in many respects a false presentation, amounting almost to a historical theory.

The same problem of selection faces the historian of economic thought, and gives him the greatest headaches. He must deal with doctrines, schools, and systems, and these are not presented as such in the material available. What is socialism? When does it begin, what are its principles and theorems? Which writers can be regarded as belonging to that system? Can we regard some writers as half or a quarter socialist? Socialism does not exist in the same sense as Marx existed.

What is the classical school? Is it, in the wide sense, the British school of thought during the Industrial Revolution, i.e., from about 1770 to 1850, starting with Adam Smith and including John Stuart Mill? Does it also include Say and Bastiat? Is Senior to be included? What are the essential principles and theorems of the school? Is it right to include Malthus and Ricardo or Say and Ricardo in the same school? Has not John Stuart Mill a separate position as a link between liberal and socialist doctrine, as a liberal socialist or a socialist liberal? Once again, the classical school does not exist in the same sense that Adam Smith or Ricardo existed.

Even when we come to a simpler problem, such as that of presenting the doctrine of Adam Smith or Karl Marx, we are still faced all the time with the drawbacks of selection. First of all, the same writer develops and changes. Take, for example, Robert Malthus. There are two essentially different editions of his *Essay on the Principle of Population:* one first published anonymously in 1798, in which the only checks to population are stated to be vice and misery, and which comes to harsh or rather hopeless conclusions, and the second edition of 1803, which, as the author himself says, "in its present shape may be considered as a new work with widely different conceptions based on the idea of 'moral restraint.'" Apart from these two editions we have the fifth and sixth editions with new additions and revisions.

There are many other instances of writers changing their views and theories. Ricardo in the third edition of his *Principles* changed his view about the effects of machinery on the interests of the workers, coming to an opinion opposite to that which he held earlier. He was dissatisfied all the time with his labor theory of value, as we see from his letters, and he eventually made a new formulation of his theory which he presented in the shorthand formula: "Labor and time." John Stuart Mill repudiated the wages-fund theory which earlier he had defended most strongly. Moreover, Mill was in later years under the influence of St. Simon and Auguste Comte. Sismondi, the critic of the classical school, in his earlier days was a follower of the classical school.

Coming to more modern writers, we find that Alfred Marshall kept changing his *Principles of Economics* all the time from one to another of the eight editions. To appreciate his teachings we have to compare all the editions, which diverge from one another in many respects.

Keynes himself was, so to speak, pre-Keynesian, Keynesian, and post-Keynesian. What is called Keynesian doctrine culminated in the year 1936 with the publication of the *General Theory,* while it is no secret that in the war years Keynes went much further in accepting the principles of planning than in his standard work.

Secondly, a writer, especially an original one, is rarely consistent. He has many sidetracks, many interests; he sees a great many aspects of the problem divergent from his main track, he does not always see clearly all the consequences of his theory, sometimes taking over the dead weight of his predecessors even when it is inconsistent with his own theory. Often he does not dare throw overboard all the cherished inheritance of the past.

Adam Smith illustrates this tendency. Even in his theory of the division of labor, the nucleus of his whole doctrine, he is not very consistent. He still thinks that agriculture is more productive than other forms of industry, that services are unproductive labor. His theory of distribution can be interpreted in various ways. He wavers between the monopolistic and physiocratic conception of the land-rent. In his theory of wages he distinguishes between different stages of economic development, taking into account different states of society, thus providing the seed for all subsequent theories of wages. He presents a theory of labor productivity, a theory of exploitation, an institutionalist theory of bargaining power, a wages-fund theory, a theory of minimum subsistence, and so on.

He shows little consistency even in his basic conceptions. We can contend that he regards labor as the mainspring and source of the wealth of nations, but we can equally well contend that he ascribes the same rôle to capital, regarding capital formation as the main factor of progress, thus making savers the chief "benefactors of society."

The historian who takes an interest in Adam Smith as Adam Smith will point out very clearly his development, his inconsistencies, and all his sidetracks, but an economic historian who is concerned with the development of economic thought, or with the sociological and historical aspects of Smith's teaching, or with didactic purpose in the history of economic thought will pay little attention to his inconsistencies or his development, but will treat his teaching as a fully grown, developed, consistent, and compact body of thought. He will prune Adam Smith's teaching as a gardener prunes his trees and bushes, giving then an aesthetically satisfying shape. A historian gives a doctrinal form to the teachings of his writers, omitting unessential parts, emphasizing others, and bringing the essentials into focus. He reinterprets each writer, recreating with him, sometimes, while adding, even correcting and revising him; he may say, for instance, "Adam Smith probably had so-and-so in mind," or, "in modern language we should call this so-and-so." It is an unhistorical method to interpret writers of old in the light of our own time, but we cannot help doing so. The natural tree is a wild one, spread all over the place, with plenty of dead wood, overgrown; the cultivated tree is pruned and lopped, selected, shaped according to our ideal type for a given species.

Adam Smith, of course, must be treated in different ways for different purposes. An economic historian will emphasize his opinions on economic conditions on the eve of the Industrial Revolution. A historian who is interested in the economic legislation of William Pitt's and subsequent governments will emphasize the whole of his *laissez-faire* program. An economist interested in the development of economic thought will emphasize all his inconsistencies, which served as seeds from which the subsequent divergent theories developed. An economic theorist who treats of Adam Smith for didactic purposes will present his doctrine of the division of labor in its present form.

It is not sufficiently realized that a historian of economic thought forms new material, i.e., a new economic thought. By reinterpreting and recreating old writers, he creates new versions of old doctrines, he puts "new wine in old bottles."

For instance, to present the economic views of the canonist school as a fully developed and consistent doctrine calls for a great deal of recreative effort and reinterpretation. We have to supplement some links in the chain of arguments, rearrange the arguments themselves, and draw general principles from the canonists' casuistic and casual remarks. We have to do the same with the mercantilist schools of thought, which take such divergent forms in writers of different nations and centuries. Basically we have to do the same with writers of all groups.

There are two fundamental approaches for the historian of economic thought. One of these may be called the sympathetic, the other the antipathetic. There are historians who deal with their subject writers with understanding, sympathy, and reverence. They seek to do them justice and to put their whole emphasis on what is permanent, valuable, and great in their teaching, neglecting what has proved wrong, biased, and irrelevant in them. They try to uncover everything which is potentially there, even if the writer was not fully conscious of all the potentialities of his doctrine. If they find some passages that are not clear, they interpret them to the best of their ability. Others take the opposite way. They try to point out the inconsistencies in the teachings, to lay bare all the false previsions and prophecies, and to emphasize all the erroneous statements and arguments. In a word, they concentrate on what is petty and mistaken in their author.

Any writer can give us his full share of the treasures he has collected or created in his time only if we are willing to profit from them and make use of them. We must always get out of any writer the best he has to give and judge him by his finest work. We can certainly get little profit by the opposite method.

The Predictions of the Economists

Are the economists more reliable in the prediction of future development or are their opinions on practical issues better than those of other men of common sense? A clue to this question can be found by looking backward and consulting the most outstanding economists of highest authority.

Let us give a few examples. *Adam Smith,* in spite of the accuracy of many of his judgments, set a very limited scope to the activity of joint-stock companies. He thought their further development was unlikely since they were suitable only for routine work and were generally rather harmful.

"The only trades which it seems possible for a joint-stock company to carry on successfully, without an exclusive privilege, are those of which all the operations are capable of being reduced to what is called a routine, or to such a uniformity of method as admits of little or no variation. Of this kind is, first, the banking trade; secondly, the trade of insurance from fire, and from sea risk and capture in time of war; thirdly, the trade of making and maintaining a navigable cut or canal; and, fourthly, the similar trade of bringing water for the supply of a great city." (Adam Smith, *The Wealth of Nations,* Book V, Chap. I, Part III.)

"The joint stock companies, which are established for the public-spirited purpose of promoting some particular manufacture, over and above managing their own affairs ill, to the diminution of the general stock of society, can in other respects scarce ever fail to do more harm than good." (*Ibid.*)

If the similar opinion of the modern economist in regard to nationalized enterprises has a similar weight, the nationalizers should not be too greatly worried.

Against any system of equality and poor relief *Malthus* argued that greater welfare would bring an increase in the birth rate, and would soon nullify the effects of the rising standard of living by producing greater numbers of mouths to be filled.

". . . the inevitable and necessary poverty and misery in which every system of equality must shortly terminate from the acknowledged tendency of the human race to increase faster than means of subsistence, unless such increase be prevented by means infinitely more cruel than those which result from laws of private property, and the moral obligation imposed on every man by the commands of God and nature to support his own children." (Robert Malthus, *Essay on the Principle of Population,* Book III, Chap. 3.)

"That this natural check to early marriages arising from a view of the difficulty attending the support of a large family operates very widely throughout all classes of society in every civilised state, and may be expected to be still more effective, as the lower classes of people continue to improve in knowledge and prudence, cannot admit of the slightest doubt. But the operation of this natural check depends exclusively upon the existence of the laws of property and succession; and in a state of equality and community of property could only be replaced by some artificial regulation of a very different stamp, and a much more unnatural character." (*Ibid.*)

What happened was quite the opposite. We see that larger incomes lead to fewer children, thus depressing the birth rate.

The woes of the economists regarding any attempt at social legislation or poor relief make depressing reading. "Beware, you will ruin yourself."

Again, take *Senior's* opinion on the project of allowances for children and the old during the discussion of the new Poor Law in 1834:

"I said that I thought it would be ruinous; that as to children it would legalize head money, the worst form of allowance, and that as to the old it would destroy benefit societies, and subject a large portion of the population to magisterial interference, to an extent even beyond that which now exists." (Nassau Senior, *History*, pp. 207–10).

On the struggle carried on against factory reform in England in the middle of the nineteenth century, William Cunningham writes in his *Growth of English Industry and Commerce in Modern Times* (p. 789):

"Each step was gained in the face of strong opposition, for the economic experts of the day—of whom Mr. Nassau Senior was the most effective spokesman—were clear that a reduction of hours would mean such a serious loss to the employers that the trade of the country must inevitably suffer, and the mischievous effects react on the workmen themselves. It was argued that if the last hour of work were cut down, the profit on the capital invested in plant would vanish altogether. (Senior, *Letter on the Factory Act*, p. 12.) Strong in the support of such academic authorities, the employers felt no scruple in evading the law, when they could; but the excuse was a mistaken one."

Jean-Baptiste Say, the great French economist in the times of Napoleon, writes against poor relief, warning against beneficence and charity as ruinous to the community:

"Has the man, who, by his improvidence and idleness, has fallen into poverty after having exhausted his means, any claim to help, when his very faults deprive the men whose capital supports industry, of their resources?" (Jean-Baptiste Say, *Treatise on Political Economy*, Vol. III, Chap. 7.)

The factory reform became a fact, yet the predicted ruin did not come about in spite of the academic authorities.

Ricardo used his theory of rent to oppose the Corn Laws. The constant tendency of land rent to rise with the development of population and the accumulation of wealth, he said, speaks in favor of the abolition of Corn Laws. In an advancing community profits must fall and rents rise, while wages remain the same. It is understandable that from this argument the conclusion must be drawn that there is no need to stimulate rent, which has a constant tendency to rise at the expense of profits, since wage-earners have really very little interest in the issue. Ricardo did not foresee that shortly after his death agriculture in Europe would undergo a century-long depression, the effect of the opening up of new farm lands and the cheapening of transport. Facts have disproved also two other propositions of Ricardo, that wages will remain stationary and that interest will fall in an advancing community, as English economic history teaches.

Sismondi, criticizing the principles of distribution under free enterprise, held that no other institutions in that respect are conceivable.

"The distribution of the profits of labour between those who co-operate in producing them, appears to me vicious; but it seems to me almost beyond human power to conceive of a state of ownership absolutely different from that which experience makes known to us."

But many subsequent writers of the socialist school and the subsequent historical development on the European continent have shown that to conceive and even maintain other forms of ownership is not beyond human power. Sismondi, however, had remarkable vision in his conception of social services and social legislation which were brought into being many years after his death.

John Stuart Mill said of the theory of value that by it everything was solved forever, that nothing could be added to its truth.

"Happily, there is nothing in the laws of Value which remains for the present or any future writer to clear up; the theory of the subject is complete; the only difficulty to be overcome is that of so stating it as to solve by anticipation the chief perplexities which occur in applying it." (J. S. Mill, *Principles of Political Economy,* Vol. I, p. 537, London, 1871.)

He did not foresee the enormous flood of economic literature on the subject of value, which has thrown new light on the problem. Nevertheless, the chapters on the "stationary state" and on the "probable futurity of the labouring classes" in Mill's *Principles of Political Economy* have a prophetic ring. And when we read the passage quoted below, we feel that what he said a hundred years ago has attained a full meaning only just now:

"I confess I am not charmed with the ideal of life held out by those who think that the normal state of human beings is that of struggling to get on; that the trampling, crushing, elbowing, and treading on each other's heels, which form the existing type of social life, are the most desirable lot of the phasis of industrial progress. It may be a necessary stage in the progress of civilization, and those European nations which have hitherto been so fortunate as to be preserved from it, may have it yet to undergo." (Vol. II, p. 328.)

And Mill's treatment of problems of property, how modern it is with its liberal-socialistic undertone: "Mankind are capable of a far greater amount of public spirit than the present age is accustomed to suppose possible." But he warns against the totalitarian consequences of a communistic system of property.

"The question is, whether there would be any asylum left for individuality of character; whether public opinion would not be a tyrannical yoke; whether the absolute dependence of each on all, and surveillance of each by all, would not grind all down into a tame uniformity of thoughts, feelings, and actions." (Vol. I, p. 263.)

Among the economists and social students who scored perhaps the greatest number of hits in their forecast of future trends I should name first of all *Saint-Simon*. He anticipated the powerful growth of industrial machinery and its all embracing power, adopting in 1817 the motto: "Everything by industry, everything for industry." He predicted the ascendancy of science and technology, which assume more and more power, even in spiritual and ethical domain. Political power, he said, will be transferred from the old classes to the technician, scientist, and administrator, since the nation becomes "nothing else but a great industrial society." His whole doctrine, which is a mixture of technocracy and socialism, comes near to our present-day experience. His advocacy of rationalization of industry is a remarkable feat of sound forecasting. So is his advocacy of internationalism: "Aujourd'hui, il doit se former entre les peuples de l'ouest de l'Europe une véritable combinaison d'efforts politiques." His true goal is internationalism, which, however, should be attained by steps. It was Saint-Simon who advocated political and economic union between France and Britain as the nucleus of a Western European unity which will attract other nations, especially Germany.

The warnings of *Carey* and *N. S. Patten* against the dangers of the depletion of natural resources of the country have largely come true. "The planter," said Carey in his *Principles of Social Science,* "is steadily giving more of his raw materials and receiving less in exchange for them," and this results in "exhaustion of the soil." Patten too stressed the danger of soil deterioration resulting from specialization in production of cotton, wheat, tobacco, and similar goods.

Marx's predictions of the future development of capitalism are faulty, but are not on the whole so mistaken as is commonly thought. He was a man of great vision. He was basically right in contending that capitalist development will lead towards socialism, if by socialism is meant the nationalization of basic industries, a process very far advanced in Europe. He was also right in his assertion that further development of capitalism if left to itself will lead to a sharpening conflict between capital and labor, to an increasing amplitude of industrial fluctuations, to a growing reserve army of labor. These predictions are confirmed by the developments in the interwar period, especially the figures of unemployment statistics in Germany, the United States, and Great Britain. He was right in foreseeing the process of centralization and monopolization of industry.

But in many other matters he proved to be wrong, in his views on the process of concentration of ownership, for example, and on the process of proletarianization and pauperization. The social pyramid has not assumed the shape he predicted in regard to the distribution of income. Wherever sections of the middle class have disappeared, they have been replaced in excess by newcomers: clerks, officials, engineers, shopkeepers, professional men.

Marx was basically wrong in foreseeing the growing impoverishment of the working classes, and this failure led to the theory of imperialism developed by the communists, especially Lenin and Rosa Luxemburg, thus producing one of the major corrections to Marxist theory. The fact that the workers in major countries, such as Great Britain, Germany, the United States, became constantly better off was explained as owing to their admission as partners in the process of exploitation of other workers in colonial and semicolonial countries by way of capital export and foreign trade and monopolistic control. And in this connection the term "social patriotism" was coined for all reform socialism.

Marx was also fundamentally wrong in predicting that the trend towards socialism would be seen most clearly in advanced industrial countries, such as Germany, Great Britain, and France. Actually the revolutionary changes took place in backward

31

countries; we might even say that socialism emerged as a revolution of backward countries. Here once more Lenin intervened, presenting in his theory of imperialism the other most important correction to Marxist theory. The revolutionary change will come, he said, from backward countries, because they will be exploited to an increasing degree by great powers organizing themselves as monopolistic concerns for national exploitation.

Coming to more recent times, we have a collection of most distinguished economists professing their views on planning, contending that planning means ruin, decline in efficiency and productivity, a decrease in national income. They assert, furthermore, that planning would mean complete lack of rational calculation, it would perforce involve irrational behavior. We could quote at length from a symposium, *Collectivist Economic Planning,* edited by *Professor Hayek,*[3] in which many famous economists took part. But today no serious economist holds this view, not even Professor Hayek, although he continues to oppose planning, not on economic grounds, but rather on political grounds, alleging that it will destroy freedom. He has himself described his *Road to Serfdom* as a political book.

Let us glance momentarily at the predictions of the most brilliant economist of our generation, the late *Lord Keynes.* His criticism of the policy of Bank of England in 1925 was right in foreseeing general misfortune as a result of the Bank's early return to the gold standard. He was wrong, however, in his appreciation of the economic consequences of the Versailles Treaty, and I need not enter here into this subject, which has been treated with great clarity by a French writer.[4]

The examples quoted, I think, should prove that economists

[3] London: C. Routledge & Sons, 1935.
[4] Etiènne Mantoux: *The Cartaginian Peace, or The Economic Consequences of Mr. Keynes, etc.* London: Oxford University Press, 1946, pp. XVII, 218.

would be wise to be extremely modest and restrained in giving advice on structural changes or in forecasting the future.

The Seeds in the History of Doctrines

Seeds in the history of doctrines are ideas from which in the course of time fully grown and fairly developed theories emerge. Like all other seeds of life, they are scattered through economic literature with a most profuse and liberal hand. They count for almost nothing, and they are most profuse in the most obscure and insignificant writers. Sometimes flashes of deep insight are to be found in cranks who in their reasoning or in their premises show the greatest defects. Ideas can be obtained cheaply, like seeds of even the rarest plants and flowers. What matters is the elaboration of ideas, the ability to grow a full-size and highly developed plant which is able to stand alone, erect, healthy, and strong, which can withstand wind and storm, which can impress by its beauty and harmony all who meet it. The seed-idea is a promise which sometimes is and sometimes is not fulfilled, whereas a plant exists, i.e., lives and multiplies, by itself.

Whosoever is looking for seeds should read the most obscure and unknown writers, and he will very often find to his astonishment highly original ideas which have been fully developed later. But we may find in abundance seeds of further development in great writers also, though it is sometimes difficult to tell whether the doctrines which developed later can be directly related to them.

The seeds of socialism are contained in Plato's *Republic,* although his socialism is authoritarian, ethical, aristocratic, idealist. He is the protoplast of the profuse Utopian literature which began in the sixteenth and seventeenth centuries and reached its peak in the early nineteenth century. Constantly growing, it found a

33

new and most powerful nourishment derived from other sources in a new interpretation of the so-called scientific socialism of Marx and Engels. The growth of the powerful and colorful socialistic tree with its many offshoots and branches presents a most exciting story.

The seeds of Malthus' doctrine are contained in Plato, Botero, Wallace, and Turgot, but they are scattered widely throughout the whole of social and economic literature. Meantime Malthus himself grows all the time, bringing many offshoots and new cuttings into being. He is eternally alive, stimulating comment, interpretation, criticism, and violent opposition.

The seeds of the psychological school in economics are to be found in Buridan in the fourteenth century and many other Schoolmen, in Say, Senior, and a number of others.

Adam Smith's liberalism grew from so many sources—the seeds of its origin were so widely scattered—that it is difficult to mention all the relevant names apart from Cantillon, Hume, Locke, Hutchinson. The tracts in defense of East India trade and the *Consideration* of 1701 (which already present a highly developed theory of division of labor) must be mentioned.

In turn, Adam Smith's great work contains a multitude of seeds of high quality which served well in the growth of economic ideas. Let us take for instance his theory of wages, presented in Chapter VIII of Book I, which is related in so many versions to different stages of economic and social development. The upper limit of wages, Smith says, is determined by the produce of labor, which constitutes the national recompense of labor in the original state of things. From that seed grew the productivity theory of wages. In the stage of advanced civilization, with the appropriation of land and accumulation of stock, Smith contended, rent and profit "make the deduction from the produce of the labor." From this version grew the surplus theory of wages. Next comes the institutional theory of bargaining power. Smith explains that the employers have the advantage in the dispute, since they are able to live for a long time on their "stock," besides forming a kind of tacit but constant and uniform combination. What, asks Smith, is the lowest limit of wage rates? "A man must always live by his work, and his wages must be at least sufficient to maintain him," is the answer, and from this hint was developed the "iron law of wages."

But Adam Smith's realistic mind suggests that "there are certain circumstances which sometimes give the labourers an advantage, and enable them to raise their wages above this rate. . . ." In times of "continual increase of the funds which are destined for the payment of wages," in an upward trend of development, we may expect a rise of wage rates. This is the wages-fund theory which was to be developed in the next century by John Stuart Mill and others.

The seeds of Keynes' theory of full employment are so widely scattered in the literature of mercantilist writers, Thomas Mun, Josiah Child, John Law, Lafemas, Monchrétien, and others, that it is difficult to name them all. In more recent times Sismondi, Silvio Gesell, Henry George, Major Douglas, Hobson—all these writers—defended the idea of underconsumption.

Cobden, in his Essay on *England, Ireland and America,* written in 1835, was the forerunner of Max Weber and Werner Sombart (or, in Britain, Tawney) in the theory of the close link between religion and industrial development, between Protestantism and capitalism. "Probably there is no country," writes Cobden, "in which the effects of the Catholic and Reformed religions upon the temporal career of communities may be more fairly tested than in Switzerland. Of twenty-two cantons, ten are, in the majority of the population, Catholic; eight Protestant; and the remaining four are mixed in nearly equal proportions of Protestants and Catholics. Those cantons in which the Catholic faith prevails are wholly pastoral in their pursuit, possessing no commerce or manufacturing industry, beyond the rude products of domestic labour. Of the mixed cantons, three are engaged in the manfacture of cotton; and it is a remarkable feature in the industry of these, that the Catholic portion of their population is wholly addicted to agricultural, and the Protestant section to communal pursuits. All the eight Protestant cantons are, more or less, engaged in manufactures." And quoting similar facts in France, Germany, Italy, Holland, Spain, and Ireland, he concludes: "The above facts, then, go far to prove that, in human affairs at least, the Reformed faith conduces more than Catholicism to the prosperity of nations."

Here we have more than a seed; we have a small plant of theory which was to become a potent element in our present-day view of the factors of industrial development.

If we equate a doctrine with the idea on which it is based, then Solomon is right: there is nothing new under the sun. But it is false to confound idea and doctrine. Ideas are flashes which show themselves again and again only to sink into oblivion.

The parable of the sower has nowhere a greater application than in the realm of social science. Why some seeds of economic thought have such an enormous power of growth and multiplication we shall never know. In any case, a theory's power of growth has little relation to its intellectual value; of this we are fully aware. Great intellectual works have very often had little influence, while a mixture of vision, analysis, and emotion has proved to be a powerful agency in shaping minds and practice in social life. Some doctrines, we say, have suited specially well the requirements of their age and have therefore caught on, although we can hardly define what we really mean by this statement. But others have been fully developed much before the time when they were adopted in practice, and of this a number of examples can be quoted.

The medieval doctrine presented by Thomas Aquinas and best suited to the three centuries after his time had been already formulated by Aristotle sixteen centuries earlier. John Law lived two centuries before the Germans, in 1923, put successfully into practice (in the so-called Rentenmark) his idea of a paper currency backed by land as security. Fichte's *Der Geschlossene Handelsstaat* ("Closed Economic State") of 1800 preceded by more than a century the Germanic State of Hitler. Adam Smith set forth his doctrine in opposition to the practices and institutions of his time long before liberal ideas were actually adopted, and thereby helped to shape and mold the historic reality into the new pattern his mind had visualized. Ricardo developed his theory of currency long before Peel's Act of 1844 made it the system followed by the Bank of England. Malthus lived long before neo-Malthusian practices took root, and Karl Marx long before the age of planning.

The Method Most Successfully Applied

What method is most successfully applied in economic literature? Let us take a glance at its masterpieces. Two of these are outstanding: one is *The Wealth of Nations*, which was described by Sir John Mackintosh as "perhaps the only book which produced an immediate, general, and irrevocable change in some of the most important parts of the legislation of all civilized nations." Bagehot says: "*The Wealth of Nations* had a wonderful effect. The life of almost every one in England—perhaps of every one— is different and better in consequence of it. No other form of political philosophy has ever had one thousandth part of the influence on us; its teachings have settled down into the common sense of the nation, and have become irreversible." And Cunningham, in his *Growth of English Industry and Commerce,* refers to it as "an epoch-making book." Anyway it is the intellectual fountain of the great and undying force of economic liberalism.

The other great masterpiece of economic literature is the *Capital* of Karl Marx, which Engels called the Bible of the working class. Be that as it may, it is the inspiration and source of the great movement of socialism. For nearly a hundred years Marx more than anyone else has been interpreted and reinterpreted by each generation in its own way, and the many versions of the doctrines to which he has given birth only prove his great fertility and productivity. Even his most deadly opponents drew from and fed on him.

What is common to these two great masterpieces is the method they apply, namely, the combination of historical and abstract analysis. Adam Smith's work is adorned and supplemented by many historical digressions and examples given in the text and notes of *The Wealth of Nations.* His book makes interesting reading just because it is as much historical as theoretical. "Besides its other perfections, it is one of the most entertaining of books," says Lord Brougham. The book derives its entertaining value partly also from its most acute polemic with the mercantilist school, to which one-fourth of the whole work is devoted. It is clear that Adam Smith's work had a definite purpose in view, to provide an instrument for the betterment of economic conditions and for reform of the government's policy.

Exactly the same characteristics are to be found in Karl Marx's *Capital.* This book is partly historical, partly theoretical, partly a severe polemic against his opponents. The history of the class struggle in France in the Revolutionary movement and the history of the class struggle in economic terms for higher wages, shorter hours, and better conditions of work are depicted in

Marx's work with great clarity and intensity. Marx studied first of all the multitudes of White Papers and other reports and memoranda issued during the period of struggle for social legislation in England and drew heavily upon them. The violence of his attack upon his opponents is hardly surpassed by anything in economic literature. He finds it necessary to explain that his attacks on the capitalists are impersonal; that he had in mind the system, not the persons of its exponents.

It is clear, and this is confirmed by Marx's utterances about himself, that the book had one overriding purpose, namely, to provide the intellectual weapon in the class struggle against the power of capital. Marx is at his best when dealing with historical development; his static theorems were weak and unconvincing. He describes the laws of capitalist development and generalizes the trends of historical change in class relations, finding a formula which runs from slavery, villeinage, long-contract labor, free and wage labor to trade-unionism and socialism. His visions are only a projection into the future of historical trends.

There are other great books in economics. Malthus' *Essay on the Principle of Population,* Ricardo's *Principles of Political Economy and Taxation,* Sismondi's *Nouveaux Principes,* Frederick List's, Roscher's, and Schmoller's works.

Malthus was one of the few economists whose name stands for a whole movement and school of thought. He has fertilized the minds not only of economists but also of naturalists, among whom Charles Darwin is the best known. Darwin himself stated: "In October 1838, that is fifteen months after I had begun my systematic enquiry, I happened to read for amusement Malthus on Population, and being well prepared to appreciate the struggle for existence which everywhere goes on from long-continued observation of the habits of animals and plants, it at once struck me that under these circumstances favourable variations would tend to be preserved, and unfavourable ones to be destroyed. The result of this would be the formation of new species."[5] It gave also to Alfred Russel Wallace "the long-sought clue to the effective agent in the evolution of organic species." The same influence of Malthus was felt by Herbert Spencer, who wrote his famous article on *The Development Hypothesis* in 1852. What is called Social Darwinism is really an offshoot of Malthusianism. Malthus influenced not only literature but also the sex and marriage behavior of the masses, as witness the neo-Malthusian movement. On examining his work we find once more the fine admixture of analysis and historical description strengthened in the later editions.

Simonde de Sismondi's *Nouveaux Principes*[6] stands at the crossroads of three great movements, influencing them enormously: the historical school, the Christian reform school of Le Play, and the socialist school. He may be regarded as the forerunner of all three. Sismondi was primarily a historian, the author of the monumental *Histoire des Français,* and his book makes great use of historical description. "Since my article published in the *Edinburgh Review*," he writes, "I have read little of economics but studied the historical facts and they have made me alter my views formerly expressed." His works make very topical reading today, anticipating the economics of national income based on adequate consumers' expenditure, the policy of full employment, and social welfare.

Frederick List's *Das nationale System,*[7] which revived the strong protectionist movement on the Continent, especially in Germany, is much more a historical treatise than a theoretical book. He

---

[5] *The Life and Letters of Charles Darwin.* Vol. I, p. 83.

[6] *Nouveaux Principes d'économie politique.* Paris, 1819.

[7] *Das nationale System der politischen Oekonomie,* Bd. T. Stuttgart & Tübingen, 1841.

writes in the same vein as Sismondi: "Since I left Germany, I have had little opportunity to study economic books, but I have studied the greatest economic book which can be studied in the U.S.A., namely the economic life of that great and prosperous country."

But what of Ricardo's *Principles?* It is not so great an exception to my thesis as appears at first sight. Ricardo's *Principles* should be read in conjunction with his *Report on the High Price of Bullion* (1810), and the *Essay on the Influence of a Low Price of Corn or the Profits of Stock* (a tract against the Corn Laws, written in 1815). The *Principles* are the continuation and generalization of views already expounded there. But even the *Principles* considered in themselves are not devoid of historical examples and rich practical material. They are based on Ricardo's wide practical experience as man of affairs, and this experience he has before his mind's eye all the time. Especially is his treatment of money, credit, and international trade far from being merely abstract and deductive.

Of more recent economic literature, the great works of Marshall, Veblen, and Keynes also prove the rule that the most useful approach to economic study is provided by a combination of historical description and theory. The modern purists, i.e., the followers of so-called "pure economics," which is to say abstract economic analysis, have brought this combination into disrepute, asking each economist to choose whether he wishes to pursue economic history or economic theory. But I believe that they are wrong, and that they prove their misconception by the ostensible exhaustion of the soil on which they operate.

Legislation and Doctrine

The interplay between economic literature and economic legislation has always been so close that many historians like Ashley have treated them together. The two bodies constantly influence each other. Economic literature prepares the way for economic legislation, as did the economic tracts of the sixteenth and seventeenth centuries in France and in England; similarly, Adam Smith's *The Wealth of Nations* entered the House of Commons through William Pitt, Ricardo's *High Price of Bullion* and *Principles* were soon translated into Peel's Act of 1844, as Malthus' criticism of the Poor Laws found expression in the abolition of outdoor relief in 1834, and the Fabian tracts soon brought a rich crop of social legislation.

Economic legislation on the other hand exerts a very great influence on economic literature, although this is seldom admitted by the economists. As a matter of fact economic legislation sometimes forms an integral part of economic literature, i.e., the particular Acts are pieces of economic writing very often more important than economic textbooks, monographs, or articles. The Elizabethan Statute of Artificers (1563) was an important piece of economic literature from which a whole economic doctrine can be deduced. This is also true of Colbert's *réglements*. The Poor Laws of the seventeenth and eighteenth centuries reveal more of the ideas prevalent in that age than do the tracts on poor relief published at that time. Economic legislation is very often a product of profound study and careful examination of conditions, apart from being a product of a compromise between very divergent interests, and the expression of a dominant opinion revealing the true ideas of a given age.

Legislative acts are very often preceded by reports, studies, and rejected and amended projects which are an integral part of this legislation in a larger sense, but which occupy a middle position between legislation and literature. Gresham's letter to Queen Elizabeth is a part of economic literature. The books of Nicolas Oresme and Nicolas Copernicus on monetary reform were ordered by Emperors Charles V and Sigismund I. The reports which preceded the social legislation of the thirties and forties of the last century, the amendment of the Poor Law, the shortening of the hours of work are not only highly valuable documents but also very interesting contributions to economic thought which were used by the socialist writers, especially Marx. In recent times the British White Paper on Full Employment and the Beveridge Plan for Social Security were more important pieces of economic literature than any other economic books which appeared contemporaneously with them. Drawing again from British experience, the Macmillan Report on Banking, the Reports on Imperial Preference, and many other such reports not only contain valuable material but are a highly developed body of economic arguments which often appear in a most systematic and almost academic form.

In modern times we have also the growing body of official publications produced by such international bodies as the League of Nations, the International Labour Office, the International Chamber of Commerce, the International Institute of Agriculture, and other international institutions, which have now to a great extent been taken over by the United Nations. Some of these publications are tracts on pure theory, such as Haberler's book on international depressions, or studies on international trade, on population, and so on. (As a matter of fact, these studies, conducted with enormous resources, on a collective research basis with the help of secretaries, technical assistants, and so on, utilizing all available documents and records, constitute a marked competition for single individual researchers, who are handicapped and frustrated by this rivalry. There is no sense in conducting single-handed research on one's own meager resources, if one knows that at the same time teams of workers in government departments, research institutes, and international institutions endowed with practically unlimited resources are carrying on research continuously on all possible subjects.)

Not only modern legislation and its documentation but the economic legislation of all times can be regarded as a kind of official literature, generally very brief, but implying doctrines which can be easily developed and presented in a more systematic and doctrinal manner.

This official literature exerts an important influence on the writings of economists. It is a boon to them and serves as a point of departure for their tracts and studies. The official findings are either attacked or defended, and they therefore, provide a canvas for the web of the economists' theories. The doctrine implied in them is either presented or supplemented, or revised, developed, and deepened. Adam Smith wrote because he wanted to prove that the ideas which underlay the existing and already obsolescent economic legislation of his time were false. Ricardo wrote because he wanted to amend the monetary legislation of his day. Malthus felt the same about the Poor Laws, François Quesnay about the agricultural discrimination in mercantilist legislation, and Jean-Baptiste Say about Napoleon's legislation. The greatest of the socialist writers wrote because they regarded the laws of property as harmful to society.

Many modern writers have taken existing economic legislation as the starting point of their investigation. Keynes attacked monetary legislation and monetary policy, gradually developing the ideas underlying his attack by generalizing them and giving them a more philosophical framework. Thorstein Veblen attacked the credit and property legislation of the United States, preparing the way for the technocratic movement in the thirties, but he generalized the implications of his criticism into the doctrine of the institutional school. The new economic legislation of Great Britain, starting with the Beveridge Report and the White Paper on Full

Employment, and developed afterwards by the Labour Government in the Social Security Acts, Health Service, Education Act, Housing Programme, and Nationalization Acts, is supported by, and contains, a new economic doctrine which has not yet been presented in economic literature, but which with time will certainly develop into a full-dress economic doctrine.

II

SOME HISTORICAL EXAMPLES

Ricardo and Marx

Among the great giants of political economy, two held key positions in its further development and determined decisively the course of its progress. I have in mind, of course, primarily David Ricardo and Karl Marx. The former determined the course of classical political economy, the latter that of socialist thought.

There are certain striking similarities between them. Both drew freely on British thought. Ricardo was a friend of Hume, of both the Mills, of Bentham, and of Malthus; he read and commented upon Adam Smith and other British writers. Marx sat for nearly twenty years in the library of the British Museum and read the works of the English classical school and the English White Papers. Marx as a Rhinelander combined three streams of thought: that of Germany from Hegel; that of France from the utopian Socialists, especially Saint-Simon; and that of England from the classical economists, especially Ricardo. The Rhineland was always the meeting place of three cultures, German, French, and English.

Another similarity between the two men is the status of each as refugee. From his early youth Marx was constantly on the move as a revolutionary. Expelled from Germany, he went to France; expelled from France, on the instigation of the Prussian Government, he moved to Brussels, where he wrote in conjunction with Engels the most revolutionary of the world's pamphlets, the *Communist Manifesto*. Then, expelled from Belgium, he went to France on the invitation of the Provisional Government, moved again into Germany to take part in the revolution of 1848, was again expelled from Germany, and went back to France; finally he came to hospitable England to settle there for good and to be buried there in Highgate Cemetery. In him was repeated the experience of the eternal refugee and stranger, constantly on the move.

Ricardo, British by birth, settled down finally as a landlord, buying a seat in the House of Commons, respectable and respected; but he was the descendant of many generations of refugees, a scion of a Spanish-Jewish family expelled by Torquemada from Spain, which moved through Italy, France, and the Netherlands, to Britain, to which Ricardo's father came. The status of refugee must have left its mark on the mind of young David, imparting to him the feeling of restlessness and insecurity against which he struggled all his life.

But here the similarity between the two men ends. Ricardo writes as a retired wealthy businessman; his aim is to give advice to the government, to the Chancellor of the Exchequer, to the Governor of the Bank of England, to merchants and industrialists. Marx writes as a revolutionary whose aim it is to forge an ideological weapon for the proletariat in its struggle for liberation. He writes deliberately for the workers and their representatives, not for the businessman or the government.

47

Ricardo's book is an expression of commercialism, of the defense which uses money as a weapon against insecurity of position. He sees economy as an auction room or as a Chamber of the Stock Exchange, where things are sold for the highest bid and all goods are transferable and movable. Marx, in contrast, is the expression of Messianism, of its search for the salvation of mankind, which is to come at the end of our days and to bring mankind out of the realm of necessity into that of freedom. As Engels, his friend and close collaborator, said:

"The objective external forces, which have hitherto dominated history, will then pass under the control of men themselves.

"It is only from this point that men, with full consciousness, will fashion history. It is only from this point that the social causes set in motion by men will have, predominantly and in constantly increasing measure, the effects willed by men. It is humanity's leap from the realm of necessity to the realm of freedom."

But the understanding of the position of the underdog and sympathy with the oppressed and downtrodden finds full expression in both writers.

It is extraordinary to find that Ricardo, the founder of commercial *laissez-faire* economics, could place so invaluable a weapon in the hands of the enemies of capitalist economy. The socialist movement fed on his heart and brains. The socialist school of thought, from William Thompson (the author of the *Inquiry into Distribution of Wealth Most Conducive to Human Happiness,* 1824), to the Fabians, the Webbs, and Bernard Shaw, was based upon Ricardo's labor theory of value. Henry George and the land reformers based their theories on Ricardo's theory of rent.

Ricardo initiated the conception that not the production of wealth, as Adam Smith contended, but its distribution forms the real object of economic study: "To determine the laws which regulate this distribution is the principal problem in Political Economy," he writes in the Preface of his *Principles*. If once we admit that the distribution of wealth is the main subject of study, then we enter fully into what may be called "social economics" of the kind advocated later by the socialist school. We cannot then avoid considering the problem of optimum distribution of income, the study of the relation of distribution to production and to human happiness.

Ricardo, the landlord, shows the position of the landlord in an awkward light. His land-rent increases constantly with the density of population or with industrial development and hence the landlord taxes his fellow citizen without contributing to their well-being. And what is the position of the wage-earner? His wage is always kept at the minimum level of existence, the rest of his labor value being divided between capitalist and landlord. We have here the first precise formulation of the "iron law of wages," the theory of exploitation.

Ricardo was most eager to revise and correct his original view that machines are not harmful to the laborers' interests, stating publicly that in this respect he had erred, that machines can really lower the gross revenue of society, if one has in mind the workers' income. This he confirmed the workers' opinion that machines compete with hands and lower their share.

How gloomy is the picture of future development drawn by Ricardo! The optimism of Adam Smith has gone, and the pattern of distribution assumes the characteric feature of class distribution and class exploitation, although the term class is not explicitly mentioned. We have only to read Ricardo's work with a sharpened eye for reference to social injustice to translate all his theorems into socialistic theory. Ricardo, not Marx, was the first to forge the theoretical weapons in the struggle of the working classes.

On reading Ricardo one wonders—Was he really a sincere believer in capitalism or *laissez-faire* economics, or did he merely pretend to be so, smuggling in ideas which were to be taken over and developed by his successors who did not have the inhibitions of a wealthy merchant and a landlord?

Modern historians of economic thought are unanimous in agreeing that without Ricardo there would have been no Marx, that there is a direct line of succession from the one to the other. Marx, who thought highly of Ricardo in contradistinction to the other economists, quotes with approval in the Preface to the second edition of his *Capital* the opinion of Professor A. Siebert, of the University of Kiev, that Marx's theory of value "is a necessary sequel to the teaching of Smith and Ricardo."

There are so many similarities between Ricardo's and Marx's theories of value that it is worth while examining them more closely, in order to see their points of convergence and divergence.

The principle of One-ness, the cornerstone of Judaism, is expressed in the work of both men. Each looks for the permanent and highest principles which underlie all the changeable movements and varieties of phenomena. This is illustrated by what Ricardo wrote to Malthus:

"My object was to elucidate principles, and to do this I imagined strong cases, that I might show the operation of these principles.

"You have always in mind the immediate and temporary effects of particular changes, whereas I put these immediate and temporary effects quite aside, and fix my whole attention on the permanent state of things which will result from them."

Marx thinks in the same way, even overreaching himself to such an extent that real prices are put aside, regarded merely as a transitory and unimportant phenomenon of the permanent laws of value. The problem of value is one thing, while the exchange relations are another thing, and both orders coincide only as an average in an over-all framework. Appearance speaks against Marx's law of value, but behind the appearance there is a deeper significance.

"The vulgar economist has not the faintest idea that the actual everyday exchange relations need not be directly identical with the magnitudes of value. The point of bourgeois society consists precisely in this, that *a priori* there is no conscious, social regulation of production. The reasonable and the necessary in nature aserts itself only as a blindly working average. And then the vulgar economist thinks he has made a great discovery when, as against the disclosures of the inner connection, he proudly claims that in appearance things look different. In fact, he is boasting that he holds fast to the appearance and takes it for the last word."[1]

Both Ricardo and Marx struggled throughout their whole life with their respective theories of value, defending them before themselves and others, not very satisfied with their results, and constantly revising them. And each regarded his theory of value as the foundation on which his whole doctrine stands or falls.

Let us now glance at the similarities and differences in these theories of value. Both regard the value of a commodity as being determined and measured "almost exclusively" by the labor-time or the "comparative quantity of labor expended on each." But here the similarity virtually ends. Ricardo treats his theory of value as a natural law valid for all stages of civilization, while Marx treats his only as the law of capitalist production, i.e., as valid historically for a certain phase of economic development.

Ricardo regards the *marginal* labor bestowed upon production of commodities as the determining factor, i.e., labor "expended in the most unfavorable conditions" necessary to "carry on the production." Marx, however, considers the "socially necessary

---

[1] Marx in his letter to Kugelman, July 1868. Karl Marx and Friedrich Engels, *Selected Correspondence*, p. 247. London: Martin Lawrence, Ltd., 1934.

labour-time" as the determinant, i.e., that required under normal conditions, which may be interpreted as the average labor-time in the industry or labor-time in the representative firm, but not as marginal labor-time.

Ricardo regards all labor as a value-determining factor; Marx, only labor expended in the process of production—labor expended in the process of circulation, such as the labor of transport workers or merchantmen, retailers, advertisers, and others, is excluded in the formation of value.

Ricardo solved his difficulties connected with the existence of capital and its different composition in time (constant and circulating capital) by the introduction of several cases in which exceptions to the rule are treated, and which led him to a higher formula: "labor and time" of production as determining factors. Marx solved the same difficulties by introducing an unexpected mechanism—the pooling of all the different rates in the organic composition of capital—i.e., by disposing of all differences and restoring an average organic composition of an artificial nature.

Ricardo, needless to say, is more realistic than Marx and far superior to him in his treatment of the complex phenomena of value. His casuistics display an ideal simplicity and are child's play compared to the casuistics of Marx, which have an air of scholastic or Talmudic tradition.

But the intellectual endeavors and achievements of both are extremely high. They sought to pierce the complex and changing surface of the troubled waters of economic life in order to reach the deep currents of life, giving expression in their cool manner, through figures and measures, to the deeper aspirations of man in order to base exchange relations upon labor relations, and in order to introduce value judgments into the field of economics, even though, it may be, they were not always conscious of these endeavors in their theoretical work.

Lenin and Marx, or the Revolt of Backward Countries

We seldom find a more perfect example than Lenin of the great disciple of a great master who is entirely devoted to the interpretation, development, and perfecting of his teacher's doctrine, entirely absorbed by one thought, one idea, one enthusiasm, one love: to be worthy of his master, to act as he would wish him to act, to defend the purity of his doctrine from debasement and defilement, and to see it established on earth in its most perfect form. Lenin regarded himself primarily as the inheritor and executor of Marxist thought. He was the St. Paul of the Marxist Church. If Lenin, then, was the father of the October Revolution, Marx deserves to be called its grandfather.

Lenin was only thirteen when Marx died. The two never met in the relationship of master-and-disciple; Lenin's apprenticeship in the craft of revolution was established through the most careful and sympathetic study of Marx's writings. His first contribution to public life in Moscow in 1893 took the form of an exercise book, *On Markets,* written in order to clarify Marxist thought as then presented by a Petersburg Marxist. How often did Lenin reverently visit the cemetery in Highgate! His wife Krupskaya in her *Memoirs of Lenin* records how, "We also liked going to Primrose Hill because it was near the cemetery where Karl Marx was buried."

Lenin made a lifelong study of Marx, reading his works again and again, consulting his teaching on every subject in a spirit of complete—we might say mystical—unity with him, often, and at every stage of the Revolution, deriving from him guidance for further action.

Nicolas Lenin and Karl Marx had many points of physical resemblance. Both had the same Socratic forehead, the same stubborn and self-willed expression, though the face of one was that of a Russian noble with Mongoloid traits, the face of the other that of a Jewish Rabbi but also with some Mongoloid characteristics. Both had undoubtedly an oriental strain. Rosa Luxemburg described Lenin as having "a real Russian peasant's head with a few faintly Asiatic lines."

Both were active against a background of hostility and hate, both lived a long way from their native land, both were refugees, for a while even in the same city. But Marx died an alien in London; Lenin was buried by his own countrymen in a splendid mausoleum with innumerable laurel wreaths.

Both believed in the same thesis: "He who is not with us is against us," and both had a strong tendency to heresy-hunting. Both were good haters, terrible against all, even those nearest to them, who seemed to them to deviate from the straight line as they themselves traced it.

Both devoted their whole life to the struggle for the emancipation of the working class, and this devotion was marked by the utmost self-abnegation. Both show a unique consistency in their multitude of books, pamphlets, speeches, articles, and notes. With both, one basic idea is developed and presented from different aspects or in different applications.

Marx once played a game with his daughters, which consisted of giving spontaneous answers to questions. Each player had to answer at once all the questions put to him. Marx's own answers to the questions asked of him were as follows:

Your most beloved virtue: Simplicity.
Your most beloved virtue in man: Strength.
Your most beloved virtue in women: Weakness.
Your most characteristic feature: Serving one idea.
Your idea of happiness: To fight.

Your idea of unhappiness: Subjection.

The quality you hate the most: Servility.

Your most beloved occupation: Being a bookworm.

This game is quite revealing; and most of these qualities revealed apply also to Lenin. Marx was a bookworm making a revolution. He presented a unique combination of a bookish man and a man of action. But he never regarded study as an object in itself. It was for him an instrument, or rather a weapon, in the fight for the emancipation of the working class. He regarded his theory as merely the forging of weapons; hence his materialistic conception of science and learning. Both Marx and Lenin were fighters and thinkers, but Marx was primarily a thinker and but for his books would remain in obscurity; while Lenin was primarily a fighter who but for his political struggles would probably be passed over by the historian with a casual remark. But both believed in the revolutionary theory as the basis and source of the revolutionary movement. "Without a revolutionary theory," said Lenin, "there can be no revolutionary movement."

But Marx had no alternative to sitting in the British Museum library, for the German Revolution in which he took an active part was a failure. Lenin did the same in his long period of exile, studying philosophy, history, sociology, and economics, and writing philosophical dissertations such as *Materialism and Empirio-Criticism: critical notes concerning a reactionary philosophy* (1909), when it was necessary to defend historical materialism from the "poisonous venom" of the "Machian traitors."

"There is nothing I would like so much, there is nothing that I have hoped so much as an opportunity to write for the workers," wrote Lenin to Axelrod from his exile in Siberia in 1897. And Lenin always found time for writing, which he regarded as the most important weapon in the revolutionary struggle, in making communism accessible and understandable to the masses. Even in the midst of his busiest revolutionary period in November 1918, when he was already the leader of Russia, he found time to write a polemical book against the Second International under the title *The Proletarian Revolution and Kautsky the Renegade.*

Both Marx and Lenin organized a party, Marx the First International, Lenin the Bolshevist Party and the Third International; but in this regard Lenin was much more successful, founding his Bolshevik Party on a professional basis and reducing and suppressing the intellectuals in the Party committees. Of course the International with all its wings organized by Marx could not achieve so great a unity and striking power as a purely Russian party organized by Lenin on a professional basis for particular and well-defined purposes.

Both had boundless faith in their cause, never wavering, never losing their conviction that it would triumph, even in their own day.

Lenin regarded as his primary task the preservation of the Marxian heritage pure and undefiled. Beginning with his fight against the Second International, against "social opportunism," social patriotism," and "social idealism," his basic aim was to stamp out the chauvinist, the idealist, the liberal, the opportunist and the "petty bourgeois," the intellectual variety of socialism. Lenin did not fight against conservatism, liberalism, or nationalism in their pure form; he did not fight against the capitalist theory of society. That Marx had done, and he refused to duplicate his work. His objective was to exterminate what he considered the weeds in the Marxist garden—the Mensheviks, the revisionists, Kautskyists, Vandervelldists, Fabians, and all kinds of evolutionary collectivists—by all powers at his command.

He wrote in 1915: ". . . The working class cannot attain its world-revolutionary object without waging a ruthless war against such apostasy, such backbonelessness, such subserviency to opportunism, and such unparalleled vulgarisation of Marxism."[2]

He continues in the same pamphlet: "By means of obvious sophism the living revolutionary soul is ripped out of Marxism, in which everything is accepted except the revolutionary methods of struggle, their propaganda and preparation, and the education of the masses for that purpose." To preserve this revolutionary soul in Marxism was his historical task. "Kautsky has turned Marx into a liberal," he argues; that is what must be prevented.

But it would be wrong to say that Lenin interpreted Marx, as a schoolman would do, in a literary fashion. He quotes with approval the statement of Engels that "our doctrine is not a dogma but a guide to action"—namely, to revolutionary action. Marx must be interpreted in a revolutionary spirit; every other way of interpretation would be false. And his exhortations to his party comrades always have the same refrain: "By all means a more revolutionary programme and more revolutionary tactics."

If we can speak of Leninism, its substance can be seen first of all in a systematic attempt to "study new situations and problems in the light of the experience of the revolutionary struggle of the world proletariat, to apply Marxist method to the analysis of new concrete situations," and Marx's writings were for Lenin only the most perfect way of teaching this method.

Marx's analysis in Lenin's view consisted in providing sweeping over-all pictures of the world situation, "a general context of political and economic relations," through the analysis of class relations. Marxist dialectic enabled Lenin to see the whole and all its details

---

[2] *Against the Stream.* A collection of articles. 1918. All quotations from Lenin in this chapter are from *Collected Works of V. I. Lenin,* authorized by the Lenin Institute in Moscow. London: Martin Lawrence, Ltd., 1929–1945.

in their proper context, while "one of the principal mistakes bourgeois economists make is that they tear particular facts, small details and figures from the general context of political and economic relations."[3] And he ends his first great work, *The Development of Capitalism in Russia*, by making this criticism of the economist (which he will afterwards repeat in relation to many of his other adversaries): "The bourgeois economist is overwhelmed by the mass of raw material and utterly incapable of appreciating its meaning and importance." He "copies the superficial, the fortuitous, the chaotic," he "counts the separate trees without seeing the wood." Only through Marxism, through the analysis of class relations can one grasp the totality, the pattern of social and economic movement as a whole.

The Marxist doctrine, says Lenin,[4] is omnipotent, complete and harmonious, and provides men with an integral world conception. ". . . Its strength consists of providing a *Weltanschauung,* guidance to action, and pattern of social economic development of one over-all conception. . . . The main thing in the doctrine of Marx is that it brings out the historic role of the proletariat as the builder of a Socialist society." And Lenin makes the following statement and prediction: "Each of the three great periods of world history since the appearance of Marxism (I: 1848–71; II: 1872–1904; III: 1904 up to the time of writing in 1913) has brought Marxism new confirmation and new triumphs. But a still greater triumph awaits Marxism as the doctrine of the proletariat in the period of history that is now opening." Lenin not only predicted this, but made it come true.

Lenin's preoccupation was always with how to grasp the future, because he was always concerned about the future, not about the present or the past. And he found only one clue as to how to grasp

---

[3] *New Data on the Laws of Development of Capitalism in Agriculture.*
[4] *The Three Sources and Three Component Parts of Marxism,* 1913.

the problems of the future: the Marxist dialectic, which in his view was "the doctrine of development in its fullest and deepest form, free from one-sidedness. The doctrine of the relativity of human knowledge which provides us with a reflection of eternally developing matter."[5] Again, Lenin said that dialectic is "a living many-sided knowledge (with the number of sides eternally increasing) with an infinite number of shadings of every sort of approach and approximation to reality" (*On Dialectics,* 1915). Not prophecies, not even the prophecies of Marx, could help him, but one thing was invaluable in Marxist armor: the revolutionary dialectic which expressed the manifold age-long experiences "of the revolutionary struggle of the world proletariat."

Lenin paid the greatest attention to the tactics of the class struggle of the proletariat conceived on the principles of comprehensive dialectical and materialistic philosophy. This tactic he sums up in a sentence derived from the *Communist Manifesto,* which reads as follows:

"The Communists fight for the attainment of the immediate aims, for the enforcement of the momentary interests of the working class, but in the movement of the present, they also represent and take care of the future of that movement."

There are two important economic works of Lenin: *The Development of Capitalism in Russia* (1899), which he began in prison and completed in Siberia, an "analysis of the social and economic system, and consequently of the class-structure of Russia in its pre-revolutionary days," and *Imperialism, the Highest Stage of Capitalism,* written at Zurich in 1916, which attempts to present "a complete picture of world capitalist economy and its international relations at the beginning of the twentieth century, on the eve of the first world imperialistic war." Both works are nothing else but

---

[5] Marx defined it as "the science of the general laws of motion—both of the external world and of human thought" (Ludwig Feuerbach).

"translations of Marxism into the language of Russian life," a kind of application of Marxism for the East.

Lenin conceived his life-task as not only to keep Marx pure and undefiled and to bring his dialectic to fulfillment, but also to bring Marx into contact with Russian life, to graft him on the Russian tree, to assimilate him into Russian thought and action. And already in his early youth Lenin started his greatest book on economics—*The Development of Capitalism in Russia,* an erudite work on economic history, based on Marxist method, containing a great wealth of statistical material presented in Marxist fashion. In this book Lenin tries to show that capitalism is not a Western system merely, but has its full counterpart in Russian life. The whole book seems to say to the Russians: *De te fabula narratur.* Capitalism and its dialectical antithesis, socialism, are not Western inventions; they have a deep historical meaning for Russia.

In that sense he speaks in his last chapter of "The Mission of Capitalism," i.e., "its historical rôle in the economic development of Russia." "To admit that this rôle is a progressive one is quite compatible . . . with the fullest admission of the negative and gloomy sides of capitalism, with the fullest admission of the inevitable, profound and all-sided social antagonism which are a feature of capitalism and which reveal the historically transitional character of this economic system." He makes the same contentions as does Marx as to the constant transformations and contradictions brought about by capitalism, i.e., centralization, concentration, proletarianization, monopolization, expropriation and pauperization. And he concludes that the Marxian analysis holds good also for Russia and sheds light on the questions of Russian development. The rate of growth of Russian capitalism, concludes Lenin, is slow, but the slowness is due to specific Tsarist institutions devised to retard it.

The study of agriculture and the problems of the Russian peasantry were the real starting-point of what is called Leninism. Has a revolutionary proletarian movement a chance in a peasant country? Is it true, as the critics of Marxism contended, that the laws of capitalist development do not hold good for agriculture, while agriculture does not diminish its share in the national economy? A mass of books, articles, speeches, and notes is devoted to this theme, and they seek to show on the basis of statistical material from all progressive countries the validity of Marxist laws in agriculture. Lenin puts forward the contention,[6] which he repeated afterwards[7] for the United States of America, that even Denmark, "the ideal country from the point of view of the opponents of Marxism on the agrarian question, reveals very clearly the capitalist agrarian system, the sharply expressed capitalist contradictions in agriculture and live-stock farming, the growing concentration of agricultural production, the elimination of small production by large-scale production, and the proletarianization and impoverishment of the overwhelming majority of the rural population."

"We observe," said Lenin, "a remarkable uniformity of evolution. . . .[8] Small production is being eliminated by large-scale production . . . The expropriation of small farming is proceeding."

Lenin understood from the outset the need for securing the support of the poor peasants in the revolutionary struggle and establishing a close "alliance between the workers and the toiling and exploited peasants." Time and again he labored hard in order to show the peasants that "there is no salvation for them except by joining in the proletarian struggle," and the workers that they should not underestimate the importance of the peasantry in Revolution. In 1905 he wrote these words, which had a prophetic ring of truth: "There is hardly another country in the world where the

[6] *Agrarian Question and Critics of Marx.*
[7] In *New Data on the Laws of Development of Capitalism in Agriculture.*
[8] *Ibid.*

peasantry is experiencing such suffering, such oppression and degradation as in Russia. The more gloomy this oppression of the peasantry has been, the more powerful will now be its awakening, the more invincible its revolutionary onslaught. It is the business of the class-conscious revolutionary proletariat to support this onslaught with all its might." The agrarian question was the weakest point in the Marxist armor, especially as to Russia, and Lenin always tried to overcome the weaknesses of Marxism.

But Lenin's contribution to Marxism was much more fundamental than mere polemics or the putting up of a system of defence for Marxism. Conceiving Marxism not "as a lifeless dogma, not a final, finished and ready-made doctrine, but a living guide to action," he realized that because of its very nature[9] Marxism "was bound to reflect the astonishing abrupt change in the conditions of social life. A reflection of the change was a profound disintegration and disunity, vacillation of all kinds, in a word, a very serious internal crisis of Marxism."

Lenin realized "the profundity of the crisis through which Marxism is passing, regarding its connection with the whole social and economic situation in the present period."[10] In his view: "The question raised by this crisis cannot be brushed aside. Nothing can be more pernicious or unprincipled than the attempt to dismiss them by phrasemongering."[11]

Moreover, this profound crisis of Marxism was a challenge to Lenin. He did not dismiss the facts contained in modern statistics, which asserted in a clear voice that the Marxist laws of pauperization and proletarianization and the Marxist forecasts of the constant drift towards economic catastrophe, the deepening economic and

---

[9] *Historical Development of Marxism*, 1911.
[10] *Ibid.*
[11] *Ibid.*

social contradictions, and the constant sharpening of economic cri-
ses are not proved by experience in Western life. The Fabians in
England, Bernstein and his revisionists in Germany, the "social
patriots" and "syndicalists" of George Sorel in France—all these
contended that the catastrophic revolutionary program of Marxism
was not borne out by actual facts, that the theory of capitalist development simply does not fit the facts. One book had to go: either
the Bible of the working classes, or the Book of Life.

Kautsky tried to give an answer to this challenge by brushing the
facts aside, explaining them away in an unconvincing and inconsistent way which only deepened the already profound crisis. At
this point Lenin took up the challenge, trying to kill three birds
with one stone: (1) to save revolutionary Marxism, (2) to anni-
hilate the "opportunists," and (3) to provide a truly Russian or
Eastern version of socialism.

He did this in his theory of imperialism, which is the crowning
achievement of his study, and which in a way opens up a new chapter in European history—one which, as Stalin said, may be called
Leninism; "Leninism is Marxism in the epoch of imperialism and
proletarian revolution."

The theory of imperialism grew out of a study of two books,
Hobson's *Imperialism* (1902) and Rudolf Helferding's *Finanz-
Kapitalismus* (1910); but the main idea had already been presented *in nuce* in the Marx-Engels correspondence and the views
expressed there on colonial questions. The influence of Helferding
can be seen in the constantly repeated term "finance capitalism" or
in the basic contention, "Monopoly has sprung from the banks"
(Chapter X), or, "Finance capital does not want liberty, it wants
domination" (quotation from Helferding).

In 1858 Engels wrote to Marx: ". . . The English proletariat is
becoming more and more bourgeois, so that this most bourgeois

of all nations is apparently aiming ultimately at the possession of a bourgeois aristocracy and a bourgeois proletariat as well as a bourgeoisie. For a nation which exploits the whole world this is of course to a certain extent justifiable." In 1882 Engels wrote in the same vein to Kautsky: "You asked me what the English workers think about colonial policy. . . . The workers gaily share the feast of England's monopoly of the world market and the colonies."

But there was another source of imperialist theory, and that, strangely enough, was provided by Cecil Rhodes' pronouncements in 1895, which are quoted in Lenin's *Imperialism:*

"I was in the East End of London yesterday," said Rhodes, "and attended a meeting of the unemployed. I listened to the wild speeches which were just a cry for 'bread, bread, bread,' and on my way home I pondered over the scene and I became more than ever convinced of the importance of imperialism. . . . My cherished idea is a solution for the social problem, i.e., in order to save the 40,000,000 inhabitants of the United Kingdom from a bloody civil war, we colonial statesmen must acquire new lands for settling the surplus population, to provide new markets for the goods produced in the factories and mines. The Empire, as I have always said, is a bread and butter question. If you want to avoid civil war, you must become imperialists."

The outline of Lenin's theory of imperialism can be presented in a few sentences: "Monopoly arose from the concentration of production at a very advanced stage of development. New and powerful monopolistic forms spread widely: combines, trusts and syndicates. Add to this a powerful development of banks. They also have turned into 'the monopolists of finance capital.' The monopolists have 'captured the most important sources of raw materials and divided the market.' Add to this the monopolies of colonial policies. To the numerous 'old' motives of colonial policy, finance

64

capital has added the struggle for the sources of raw materials, for the export of capital, for 'spheres of influence,' i.e., for spheres of good business, concessions of monopolist profits, and so on; in fine for economic territory in general."

"Naturally," said Lenin, "finance finds it most convenient to proceed with political conquest, because it is able to extract the greatest profit from a subordination which involves the loss of the political independence of the subjected countries and peoples. Colonial possession alone gives complete guarantee of success to the monopolies against all the risks of the struggle with competition, including the risk that the latter will defend themselves by means of a law establishing a state monopoly. First it was possible simply to 'grab' new territories, yet free, but when the whole world has been shared out, there was inevitably ushered in a period of colonial monopoly, and consequently a period of intense struggle for the partition and repartition of the world."

"The time of the definite victory of world finance capital" is the beginning of imperialist wars, and Lenin speaks of the war of 1914–1918 already at the time he wrote (1917) as "the first imperialist war." "The struggle of world imperialism is becoming aggravated. . . . The more capitalism develops, the more the need for raw materials arises, the more bitter competition becomes and the more feverishly the hunt for raw materials proceeds all over the world, the more desperate becomes the struggle for the acquisition of colonies.

"Monopolies, oligarchy, the striving for domination instead of the striving for liberty, the exploitation of an increasing number of small or weak nations by an extremely small group of richest or most powerful nations—all these have given birth to those distinctive features of imperialism which compel us to define it as parasitic or decaying capitalism. More and more there emerges, as one of the tendencies of imperialism, the creation of the 'bondholding' (*rentier*) state, the usurer state, in which the bourgeoisie lives on the proceeds of capital exports and by 'clipping coupons.' "[12]

Now note that the phrase "the usurer state" means that the whole community can live as a usurer, as an exploiter of other nations, its bourgeoisie not only living at the expense of the workers of other nations but corrupting their own workers with the proceeds of their "super-profits."

The imperialism of the beginning of the twentieth century completed the partition of the world among a very few states, each of which today exploits (i.e., draws super-profits from) a part of the world. . . . "Each of them, by means of trusts, cartels, finance capital, and debtor and creditor relations, occupies a monopoly position on the world market. . . ."

Embryonic imperialism, said Lenin, has grown into a dominant system; capitalist monopolies occupy first place in economics and politics; the division of the world has been completed. On the other hand, instead of an undisputed monopoly by Great Britain, we see a few imperialist powers disputing among themselves for the right to share in this monopoly, and this struggle is characteristic of the whole period of the beginning of the twentieth century.[13]

What follows from all this? First of all, if the Marxist laws of capitalist development did not come true, it is because the great industrial powers entered on a new stage in capitalist development, the stage of imperialism, which is "a stage of monopolistic and parasitic capitalism," living and expanding at the expense of other nations. The great powers exploit other countries of colonial or semicolonial character, or simply economically backward, and they admit their workers to a share in this exploitation. The working class of the imperialistic powers therefore get a higher level of wa-

---

[12] *Imperialism, the Highest Stage of Capitalism*, 1917, Ch 10.
[13] *Ibid.*, Ch. 8.

ges and employment than would be justified by the laws of surplus value operating at home. This produces a deviation of trends of development away from the lines sketched by Marx.

Secondly, and this is another facet of the theory of imperialism, Lenin explains that "social patriotism" is nothing but the reflection in thought of the new changes in real life. Imperialism created a rich soil for the growth of proletarian weeds in Marxism. There is a close "bond between imperialism and opportunism," and this bond is first and most clearly revealed in England "owing to the fact that certain features of imperialist development were observable there much sooner than in other countries." The workers are bribed subconsciously into the position of social opportunism, "receiving crumbs of super-profits," especially in those countries having a higher percentage of skilled workers than oppressed nations. "A privileged upper stratum of the proletariat in the imperialist countries lives partly at the expense of hundreds of millions of members of uncivilized nations."[14]

But this situation is only transitional because, with the inevitable breakdown of that monopoly, the working classes of those imperialistic powers will also lose their privileged position. The workers of these imperialistic powers have only a "respite" (Schonungszeit) which must soon come to an end when the mass of foreign exploitation is finished and the colonial workers impoverished, and when imperialism, leading to annexation, to increased national oppression, and consequently also to increased resistance, leads the world to destruction.

Therefore, concluded Lenin, it is our duty, if we wish to remain Socialists, "to go down lower and deeper, to the real masses," and not to remain on the surface with the leaders of the upper stratum of the working class; and also to get in touch with those members of the "uncivilized" and backward nations which form the hard

---

[14] *Imperialism and the Split in Socialism,* 1916.

core of exploited workers, where national exploitation is added to social exploitation. This is the third and most important bird caught by the great hunter from the Russian steppes.

We see then how Leninism became the Eastern version of socialism, the version of socialism for backward, agricultural, semi-colonial, and colonial countries. Here we see how Lenin combined his fundamental interpretation of Marxism in his time with his Russian aspirations, how he became the supreme theorist, the leader and organizer of the revolt of the backward countries.

Not the nationalists and Fascists, but Lenin was the first to take up and develop "the idea of dividing nations into oppressing and oppressed," and he admits in a Report[15] written in 1920 that this "thesis appeared first over his name." The characteristic feature of imperialism, he writes, is that the whole world is at present divided into a large number of oppressed nations and an insignificant number of oppressing nations possessing colossal wealth and powerful military forces. The overwhelming majority of the population of the world, numbering more than a thousand millions, in all probability 1,250 millions, if we take the total population of the world then to be 1,750 millions, i.e., about 70 per cent of the population of the world, belongs to the "oppressed nations," which are either in a state of direct colonial dependence; or belong to the outlying colonial states, such as Persia, Turkey, and China; or else, after being conquered by the armies of a big imperialist power, have been forced "into dependence upon it by treaties." And writing later in 1920 in his *Preliminary Theses* on national colonial questions he pens the following words:

". . . It is necessary steadily to explain to and expose among the broad masses of the toilers of all countries, and particularly of backward countries, the deception which the imperialist powers

---

[15] *Report* of the Commission on the National and Colonial Questions at the Second Congress of the Communist International, July 26, 1920.

systematically practise by creating, in the guise of politically independent states, states which are absolutely dependent upon them economically, financially and militarily. . . ." The age-long oppression by the imperialist powers "has imbued the toiling masses of the oppressed countries, not only with anger, but also with distrust towards the oppressing nations in general, including the proletariat of those nations."

From this it follows logically that the great proletarian revolution would come, not, as Marx predicted, in the West as the logical outcome of ripened capitalist development, but in the East, where foreign capitalism adds imperialism and accumulates misery, exploitation, and proletarianization in the oppressed nations. But Lenin never regarded this as a contradiction of the dialectic materialism of Marx condensed in the following passage:

"No social formation ever disappeared," says Marx, "before all the productive forces are developed for which it has room, and new higher relations of production never appear before the material conditions of their existence are matured in the womb of the old society. . . . The organisation of the revolutionary elements as a class presupposes the finished existence of all the productive forces which are developed in the bosom of the old society. . . . Law can never be on a higher level than the economic conditions and the degree of social civilization corresponding to it. . . . The industrially more developed country reveals to the less developed the image of its own future."

Lenin admitted that Marx had seen "the birth of the new society from the old, the forms of transition from the latter to the former as a natural historical process," but he represented himself as correcting Marx in this respect, that whereas Marx studied the laws of capitalism, as they then existed, while he, Lenin, presents the laws of imperialism, which is a new stage of development. He says expressly that "imperialism is progressive as compared with pre-monopoly capitalism" as much as "capitalism is progressive compared with feudalism."[16] It is not capitalism but imperialism that leads to socialism. It does so through the struggle of revolutionary nations and strata, and those are the ones oppressed by imperialism. Where the famine and ruin are greatest, there the capitalist domination is most likely to be overthrown and a new phase established. Thus imperialism hastens the coming of the socialist revolution by famine, anarchy, destruction. This is the correction of Marx contributed by Lenin, and this correction may be regarded as the essence of Leninism.

There is more voluntarism and less determinism in Lenin than in Marx, greater reliance upon professional revolutionists than upon automatic development and rise of the masses. Marx provided a theory for the West; Lenin for the East. Marx believed in the ripening of capitalism; Lenin in squashing it prematurely, primarily as a foreign importation of a weak and sickly nature. Marx believed in the masses; Lenin in the Party, in the class-conscious minority which leads and guides; Marx believed basically in democracy; Lenin in the dictatorship of the proletariat, i.e., the dictatorship of its organized and class-conscious minority. The belief in dictatorship was nothing but a consequence of the rejection of the doctrine of the ripeness of capitalism. If we do not wait for the ripe fruits of capitalist development, we cannot expect a socialist majority for the revolution, and Lenin was eager to show that the socialist majority in imperialistic countries may never come about, owing to the crumbs falling from the rich table of imperialist oppression.

Lenin's single motto, repeated time and again, was that it was necessary to create a "revolutionary situation," i.e., not to wait for the ripening of capitalism but to do something to hasten the ripening of imperialism, with its inevitable results of the destruction of

---

[16] *Caricature of Marxism and Imperialist Economism. Collected Works,* Vol. 5.

goods but also of social relations and positions of social power. What would Lenin say now if he were to consider a possible war between the West and Soviet Russia? I can imagine him giving ·the following answers in a purely imaginary conversation:

Q. Would you not be afraid that Soviet Russia would lose the war and communism be extinguished?

Lenin: No, because whatever happens a third imperialistic war on such a scale and with such destructive weapons as now are available would certainly bring about the climax of a revolutionary situation, and socialism would triumph all the world over, whether it be called communism, socialism, sovietism, or anything else. Soviet Russia might lose the war, but communism would win. These are the laws of capitalistic development as described by Marx with my supplement in *Imperialism.*

Q. Do you not think that socialist building is more important than creating the climax of a "revolutionary situation"?

Lenin: No, for socialist building may create a new form of opportunism, patriotism, and even imperialism, and may drive the Russian workers into the same privileged position as was formerly enjoyed by other imperialistic countries. Socialist building in a great communist empire will ultimately lead to new forms of imperialism, while world communism can only be established through creation of a world-wide, "revolutionary situation." Socialist building would mean the end of the socialist revolution, and I proclaimed "a permanent revolution." The revolution is not yet complete. We had the chance to start our revolution because the capitalists were stupid enough to wage their first great imperialist war. Stalin was able to score new triumphs because the capitalists were foolish enough to lead a second imperialist war. Now we could expect further triumphs from a third imperialist war. It would be a heaven-sent gift from the imperialists if they were to attack Soviet Russia, for then it would make our task incomparably easier; but if they were unwilling to help us, I believe Russia should do it, although she might lose the war. But Russia doesn't count; it was not our aim to make Russia great. We are not petty-bourgeois chauvinists and patriots. We work for world salvation.

Q. Do you still believe that your theory of imperialism holds good, and for how long?

Lenin: Your contemporaries are very stupid. They have completely lost the power to think for themselves, and keep on repeating the same phrases. I taught that according to Marx every doctrine is only a reflection of existing social relations; but these social relations change constantly, and it is your duty to think out for yourself a new doctrine related to the changed conditions of your life. I think the doctrine of imperialism still holds good to a certain extent, but there is a new factor which I have not taken into account in my theory of imperialism, the emergence of Soviet Russia in the fight of imperialism. This makes a great deal of difference in the historical dialectic, but it is for you to think out all the implications of this fact.

Q. Do you mean to say that you are afraid that Soviet Russia will grow into an imperialist power instead of a socialist one?

Lenin: I started the theory of imperialism with a new fact, which I had to explain: Why the majority of free people under the Western democracies in my time did not care for revolutionary socialism. And I have given my answer in my book *Imperialism.* If I were alive now, I should start my inquiry with a new fact, which is likewise very startling: Why it is that the Eastern peoples, the permanent object of Western imperialism, who are now liberated by the Soviet Union, do not like to be liberated; what it is that makes them reject communism? Is it simply ignorance, prejudice, the effect of centuries-long propaganda, or something else?

Q. Perhaps the Western imperialists give better terms to the oppressed nations than the Eastern imperialists do. You said yourself
in your book on imperialism that the imperialist powers, in order
to exploit these countries effectively, have to construct railways,
to build factories, and to establish commercial and industrial
centers in them. And now they even have to carry food and raw
materials and other aid into those countries. But Soviet Russia
does not do that; she removes stores of goods and productive equipment and concludes agreements that are not very beneficial for
the oppressed nations, perhaps because she is poor herself and
desires to become stronger and more prosperous.

Lenin: The cause of all this may be the corruption brought
about by the machinery of the state and of a great Power. You
know how I fought all my life against social patriotism, social
chauvinism, or opportunism. Now I see all these things revived
in the Soviet Union. The trouble is that all peoples prefer the
benefit of their own country to the benefit of other countries. But
this is a capitalistic or imperialistic principle. They ought to prefer the good of the cause of world socialism. If world socialism
can gain by providing countries in the Russian zone of influence
with tractors, raw materials, and industrial equipment, Russia
should send these things to those countries and not keep them for
herself. This would not be an act of abnegation or altruism, but
practical international socialism, and a better act of communist
propaganda than all the speeches of Molotov and Vyshinsky. But
all the Soviet leaders have become petty bourgeois. I have always
shown how power corrupts whole sections of the working class,
especially its upper stratum, and now I find another striking confirmation in the communist leaders. I think socialism must again
try to descend into the sphere of the lower strata, either into this
handicapped stratum of underpaid workers in the imperialist
countries or into the working class of oppressed nations. They will

be the future bearers of the triumphant colors of international socialism. Only those who suffer can bring a renewal of socialism; nothing can be expected from those who rule and misrule.

Such is our imaginary conversation with Lenin.

Mandeville, Forerunner of the Naturalists

The duality nature-nurture, or nature-morality and culture—the realm of things and realm of values—has its full counterpart in the flow of economic thought. There have been economists who were entirely absorbed by the facts of life and nature—the so-called naturalists or realists; and others who were entirely absorbed by values, ideas, and ideals—the reformers, the idealists or believers in perfectibility.

The motto of the naturalists was: It was meant to be like that, the "Invisible Hand" has so decreed. The pursuit of self-interest and individual gain is part of the great scheme of nature. Nature is the field of struggle, and the fittest survives. It is not a discovery by Malthus, but the age-long experience of all naturalists, of all observers of the ways of nature, that one species preys on another; every gardener or farmer knows that space is limited, that you must constantly choose between one plant and another, between breeding one animal or another, and that there is no equality, peace, or justice in nature. The naturalist accepts inequality, struggle, and even cruelty as necessary ingredients of life, devised to secure its permanence and even perfection, and regards himself as free from the cheap sentimentality of the reformer. He accepts life as it is and studies its laws reverently. He invariably appeals to the facts. Facts, facts, facts—they alone govern; everything else is a utopia, an illusion! The naturalist invariably says: Take man as he really is, not as he should be. Individual or class, regional or even national disadvantages do not matter;

the totality of life derives advantage from the struggle because the fittest survives, the community gets service for the lowest price, and improvement is constantly brought about by sheer force of self-interest and utility. Man "intends only his own gain, and he is in this as in many other cases, led by an invisible hand to promote an end which was no part of his intention," says Adam Smith.[17]

"To the laws of property and marriage," says Malthus, "and to the apparently narrow principle of self-interest which prompts each individual to exert himself in bettering his condition, we are indebted for all the noblest exertion of human genius, for everything that distinguishes the civilised from the savage state."[18]

It is interesting to note that the thesis is common to all naturalist economists, whether old or new, of the classical, psychological, mathematical, or neoclassical school, and we can find it even in Marshall, who stresses the law of substitution as the central law of economics, regarding that principle as an expression of a general law of the survival of the fittest.

All liberals are naturalists, whether they actually use mechanical (physical) or organic (biological) analogies. They are naturalists in the sense that they regard competition based on utility and self-interest as the expression of a general fight for survival and betterment. Thus Marshall, who as a mathematician used the formulas of mechanical equilibrium, nevertheless often used biological analogies, as for instance in Chapter VIII of his *Principles,* where, studying the competition of old and new firms, he expounds at great length the law of the survival of "the fittest" in the struggle for existence.

In modern economic literature devoted to the themes of planning, control, and socialism, we can also find the same exposition

---

[17] *The Wealth of Nations,* Book IV, Chap. II.
[18] *Essay on the Principle of Population,* Book IV, Chap. XIV.

of the naturalist's conviction that utility, self-interest, competition, and struggle are part of nature's design for the survival of the fittest and betterment, and that too much control, protection, subsidy, or charity weakens man's energy and his drive towards betterment.

It is interesting to seek out the roots of this thesis in economics, even though we cannot assign a precise or definite date for its appearance, because the doctrine has behind it an age-long experience based on the quite common view that "good springs from evil," that man rises to the heights of moral perfection when confronted with evil, or that what is evil for one may be good for the community.

"Nothing was more instrumental in forwarding the Reformation than the Sloth and Stupidity of the Roman clergy," says Mandeville, and John Law writes in his *Proposals and Reasons for constituting a Council of Trade* (Glasgow 1700), ". . . we see that in times, and with men who had a much more immediate hand of the Almighty upon them, even to such as Joseph, Moses, Gideon, David and many others, the exercise of trouble, disappointments, and afflictions were found to be indispensably necessary."

Mandeville was of course not the first who upheld this Miltonian[19] truth, but he gave it very forceful expression, and by his systematic exposition, vigorous style, and real acuteness enormously impressed the radicals and liberals, who in the age of the coming Industrial Revolution were well prepared for his *Credo*.

The roots of economic naturalism can therefore be clearly seen in the writings of Bernard Mandeville (1670[?]-1733), a Dutch-born British writer. Two things of interest may be noted about Mandeville. Firstly, he was, like François Quesnay, the first great representative and exponent of naturalism in economics, a doctor

---

[19] "Without evil there can be no good."

of medicine, which proves his interest in nature-study. Secondly, he is "said to have been hired by the distillers to write in favour of spirituous liquors." The *Dictionary of National Biography* records that Mandeville "was probably little respected outside distilling circles."

The elements of the naturalists' creed may be found in Mandeville's *Fable*, the first and shortest version of which was published in 1705 in a doggerel poem called *The Grumbling Hive or Knaves Turned Honest*, and then twice expanded, once in 1714, again in 1724.

"One of the greatest Reasons why so few people understand themselves," said Mandeville, "is that most writers are always teaching Men what they should be, and hardly ever trouble their heads with telling them what they really are."[20] For Mandeville man is "a compound of various Passions, that all of them, as they are provoked and come uppermost, govern him by turns, whether he will or no." And Mandeville's object is to show that "these qualifications, which we all pretend to be asham'd of, are the great support of a flourishing Society. . . ."

Mandeville's approach to man is like his approach to a cat or a fox or a wolf. The animal was meant to be the animal he is, he was fashioned in that way, and it is foolish to wish him to be an angel. "It is as possible that cats, instead of killing rats and mice, should feed them and go about the house to suckle and nurse their young ones; or that a kite should call the hens to their meal, as the cock does, and sit brooding over their chickens instead of devouring 'em; but if they should do so they would cease to be cats and kites; it is inconsistent with their natures and the species of creatures which now we mean, when we name cats and kites, would be extinct as soon as this could come to pass."

"The first desirable Blessing for any Society of Men is a fertile

---

[20] *Fable* (1714).

Soil and a happy Climate, a mild Government, and more Land than People." But in such a state "you need not fear great Vices, so you must not expect any considerable Virtues. Man never exerts himself but when he is rous'd by his Desires. . . ."

"Would you render a Society of Men strong and powerful, you must touch their Passions. . . . Divide the Land, tho' there be never so much to spare, and their Possessions will make them Covetous: Rouse them, tho' but in Jest, from their Idleness with Praises, and Pride will set them to work in earnest. Teach them Trades and Handicrafts, and you'll bring Envy and Emulation among them. . . . Teach 'em Commerce with Foreign Countries, and if possible get into the Sea, which so compass spare no Labour nor Industry, and let no difficulty deter you from it: Then promote Navigation, cherish the Merchant, and encourage Trade in every Branch of it; this will bring Riches, and where they are, Arts and Sciences will soon follow. . . ."

And in another context Mandeville writes:

"The great Art . . . to make a Nation happy and what we call flourishing, consists in giving everybody an Opportunity of being employed; which to compass, let a Government's first care be to promote as great a variety of Manufactures, Arts and Handicrafts, as Human Wit can invent; and the second to encourage Agriculture and Fishery in all their Branches, that the whole Earth may be forc'd to exert itself as well as Man; for as the one is an infallible Maxim to draw vast multitude of People into a Nation, so the other is the only Method to maintain them.

"It is this Policy, and not the trifling Regulations of Lavishness and Frugality . . . that the Greatness and Felicity of Nations must be expected; for let the value of Gold and Silver either rise or fall, the Enjoyment of all Societies will ever depend upon the Fruits of the Earth, and the Labour of the People; both which joyn'd together are a more certain, a more inexhaustible and a more real Treasure than the Gold of Brazil, or the Silver of Potosi. "Diligence and Industry are often used promiscuously, to signify the same thing . . .", but "Industry implies besides the other qualities a thirst after gain, and an Indefatigable desire of meliorating our Condition."

Mandeville stresses the point that mass poverty is a natural phenomenon, beneficial to society as a whole, which must be kept in being permanently, warning before Malthus did against poor laws and the charity system. Men in his view are "more prone to Ease and Pleasure than they are to Labour, when they are not prompted by Pride or Avarice, and those that get their Living by their daily Labour, are seldom influenced by either: so that they have nothing to stir them up to be serviceable but their wants which it is Prudence to relieve, but Folly to cure. The only thing then that can render Man industrious, is a moderate quantity of Money; for as too little will, according as his Temper is, either dispirit or make him Desperate, so too much will make him Insolent and Lazy."

Mandeville advises keeping the poor in poverty, because "it would be easier, where Property was well secured, to live without Money than without Poor; for who would do the work? For this reason the quantity of circulating Coin in a country ought always to be proportion'd to the number of Hands that are employ'd; and the wages of Labourers to the price of Provisions."

These are the beliefs which are roots of the classical doctrine. Both Adam Smith, who devoted a whole chapter to Mandeville under the title "Of Licentious Systems," and Malthus, who likewise does not approve of Mandeville[21] do in fact put Mandeville's wine into new bottles with new, more systematic and "scientific" labels.

---

[21] "Let me not be supposed to give the slightest sanction to the system of morals inculcated in the Fable of Bees, a system which I consider as absolutely false." (*Essay on the Principle of Population*, 4th ed., p. 492, note.)

Marx and Keynes

Perhaps the most striking differences between the doctrines of Marx and those of Keynes consist in the ways each approaches the subject. Marx would call his own method dialectical; Keynes's method is rationalistic and analytical. Marx detects contradictions inherent in the capitalist system which must lead to a next and higher stage in economic organization, whereas the flaws Keynes sees can be remedied within the same system. Keynes is a doctor of capitalism; Marx is its gravedigger.

Keynes deals basically with the more static forces of economics and small changes; Marx with the dynamic forces, big changes, transformations, and developments. Keynes's *General Theory,* in its way of exposition, resembles the great Marshallian textbook because it was meant to be a polemic against the Marshallian school, while *Das Kapital* is similar to the great historical and sociological treatises of the socialist thinkers regarded by Marx as his rivals. Keynes avoids value judgments and broad structural issues and moves within the existing institutional framework, whereas Marx enters the broader system of values, and his analysis often transcends the framework of existing institutions. Both aim at a certain economic philosophy, but Marx aims at it directly, leading the assult on the basic system of values on a broad front, while Keynes aims at it only indirectly. In fact more was done in that respect by his followers than by himself, so that the gap between Keynes and the Keynesians was perhaps even greater than the gap between Marx and the Marxists. Marx presents an antithesis to capitalism, while Keynes aims at synthesis between capitalism and socialism in a Cambridge version of welfare economics, in many ways already orginated by Marshall.

In spite of these dramatically opposed ways of approach adopted by Marx and Keynes there are some astonishing similarities in the treatment of the same subject, the critical analysis of capitalist

production. For both Keynes and Marx attacked the same problem—the deficiency of purchasing power and the failure of the
economy to provide employment for people anxious to work, a
situation leading to accompanying wastage, destitution, and
misery.

Marx presents his "critical analysis of captitalist production"
under the formula, M(oney): C(ommodity): M(oney). The
capitalist, the central figure in his *Capital,* invests money in producing commodities in order to get more money. He is singled
out in the process of circulation of values, placed outside the equa-
tion of exchange, one side of which is his purchase price, the other
his selling price. The capitalist pays out a certain amount of value
in his process of production and claims more value on the market.
The difference is his profit or profit-like income in the form of
rents and interest, all of which is covered under the term "surplus
value." But whence comes this surplus value? Marx tries to show
that it cannot arise in the process of circulation (among the capitalists themselves) but must arise in the process of production,
springing from the fact that the price of labor (equivalent to the
value of the means of subsistence of the worker) is below its use
value, which is the product of the worker's labor.[22]

But how can capitalists as a class extract more money than they
pay out? Here is the basic cause of the disequilibrium of the capitalist system, the roots of its contradictions. It is the source of a
basic deficiency in effective demand, since income generated by
the capitalist for the services he enlists is below the selling value
which he must extract for his output.

---

[22] Marx, *Capital,* Vol. I, p. 145. "In order to be able to extract value from the
Consumption of a commodity, our friend, Moneybags, must be so lucky as to find,
within the sphere of circulation, in the market, a commodity, whose use value
possesses the peculiar property of being a source of value, whose actual consumption therefore, is itself an embodiment of labor, and, consequently, a creation of
value."

The system might work in two ways: one unrealistic way, covered by the "formula of simple reproduction"—the capitalist consumes his entire profits (at zero investment rate) ; the other realistic way, covered by the "formula of extended reproduction" —the capitalist pays out the difference between his profit and his consumption in the form of investment ("reproduction on a progressively increasing scale"). The capitalist equilibrates the deficiency of effective demand dynamically by injecting more money into his investments. The accumulation of real capital, or of foreign investment (the theory of imperialism), or of gold makes the whole system workable. Therefore the motto of the capitalist system is: "Accumulate, accumulate!" "Reconvert the greatest possible portion of surplus value, or surplus product into capital."

Investments equilibrate the system dynamically, but only over a short period, and the whole analysis of Marx is designed to show that this fever of investment leads the whole system to a catastrophic end, because the cause of disequilibrium is not removed but delayed, while the disequilibrium is growing all the time through the effect of investment on productivity of labour.

"The mass of the surplus increases." "Hand in hand with the increasing productivity of labor goes . . . the cheapening of the worker, therefore a higher rate of surplus value" and constant replacement of labor by the machine (the growth of the industrial reserve army).

The movement by which the system can be kept working must become even more speedy, until it becomes delirious and breaks down. The cause of the final breakdown is the constant growth of the relative surplus value,[23] which widens the gap between po-

---

[23] It is surplus value growing with productivity of labor. "The surplus-value produced by prolongation of the working day I call absolute surplus-value. On the other hand, the surplus-value arising from curtailment of the necessary labour-time and from the corresponding alteration in the respective lengths of the two components of the working day I call relative surplus-value." *Capital*, Vol. I, Part 4, Ch. 10.

tential and actual production and which must be bridged by new investments with all their destructive force on the labor market.

The existence of profit makes the whole system unworkable; without it any potential output could be sold fully to the consumers without need for investments for their own sake, because then output would equal wage, value would equal consumers' expenditure.

Lord Keynes's approach to the same problem of deficiency of effective demand is basically different from Marx's in that it does not single out the entrepreneur in the formula of circulation of values. Profits are treated in the same way as "factor costs," i.e., "amounts paid by the entrepreneur to the factors of production (exclusive of other entrepreneurs) for their current services." The problem of whence comes the entrepreneur's profit is at once dropped as nonexistent. This profit is part of income as is anything else. Factor cost plus entrepreneur's profit is the total income resulting from employment given by the entrepreneur, and the aggregate sum of total income is equivalent to the value of national output. This value by definition provides an effective demand exactly equal to the value of output, provided that the whole income is spent on goods and services. There is no deficiency in the process of production as alleged by Marx; the deficiency arises in the sphere of circulation when part of income for one reason or another is not spent on goods and services. The deficiency is created by voluntarily withholding part of total income from spending on goods and services, i.e., by saving which is not offset by investment. The whole output of a country can be sold to the "market" at the factor cost plus profit because the employment has generated income sufficient for this transaction. Saving, not profit, is the cause of disequilibrium, but in Marx's as well as in Keynes's system the workability of the system is dependent on the offsetting of the deficiency by investment. Even in a socialist society, according to Keynes, deficiency of effective demand could arise if saving were not offset by investment. It may be remarked that for Marx saving was organically linked with profits; in his time small savings were practically nonexistent, and his theory of surplus value, which determines the price of labor by the value of the worker's means of subsistence, excludes from the outset any emergence of workers' savings.

In Keynes's view the disequilibrium arises not only out of greed as in Marx's system, but out of fear, out of expectations and anticipations of individuals who wish to secure their positions by holding cash or bank deposits or other claims against members of the community, or generally by withholding purchasing power, i.e., simply by nonspending, whether on consumption or on investment. It is not the fever of investment which brings about the disequilibrium of the system but the anxiety of the savers (or the mistrust of the investors). The savers are not always the "benefactors" of the community as in Adam Smith's conception; they are certainly not the benefactors whenever they choose to save in excess of the existing investment possibilities.

Any surplus of claims of the savers as expressed in the "propensity to save" over the value of investment cannot materialize, because there is no counterpart in real wealth. The savers can only appropriate the difference from the accumulated wealth by causing dissavings of others. This means that not all individual savings are materialized for the community. What is not turned into investment is not materialized. And what is not materialized vanishes for the community, a situation that amounts to a loss of national output and unemployment.

Individuals are free to save more or less as they choose, but all individuals put together are not able to save more than they invest. The flow of individual saving and investment must be equilibrated in such a way that there is no leakage of expenditure, so that the whole income is spent on goods and services in the two segments consumption and investment.

Whenever the "propensity to save" exceeds the inducement to invest, we face a lack of purchasing power which makes impossible the sale of the total produce of the community to consumers and investors at its factor cost, and it is this impossibility which leads to the lowering of output and employment. Thus the formula is simple: "The propensity to save must be offset by investment."

In Lord Keynes's conception the capitalist system is not basically wrong and could be easily put right. "It is in determining the volume, not the direction of national employment that the existing system has broken down." The volume of employment can be easily brought to the potential maximum by more expenditure on consumption or investment. The control of the rate of investment is the remedy, and the method of conservative planning for restricted goals (the socialization of investment) is advocated. "Whilst, therefore the enlargement of the functions of government, involved in the task of adjusting to one another the propensity to consume and the inducement to invest, would seem to a nineteenth century publicist or to a contemporary American financier to be a terrific encroachment on individualism, I defend it, on the contrary, both as the only practicable means of avoiding the destruction of existing economic forms in their entirety and as the condition of the successful functioning of individual initiative."[24]

Lord Keynes shares with Karl Marx the view that the deficiency in effective demand is growing with time, because the propensity to save increases with the rise of national income. But whereas Marx, in consequence of his theory, provided a long-term analysis showing where all this development leads to, Lord Keynes

[24] J. M. Keynes, *The General Theory of Employment, Interest and Money*, p. 380.

confined himself to the short-period aspect, not bothering about the structural changes which will be brought about if the deficiency is constantly covered by new investments on an ever extending scale.

Marx did not deny that the capitalist system can work in a short period, holding only that in the long run the whole system is headed for a breakdown. Lord Keynes, showing that the capitalist system can work over a short period, does not say anything about the long-period aspect. The problem of achieving full employment has been solved theoretically and practically many times, whereas the problem of maintaining full employment in the long run has been solved neither theoretically nor practically. The problem is really how to maintain full employment, not how to achieve it.

Lord Keynes has shown that there is a monetary answer to the problem of unemployment, but the problem has much more than a monetary aspect—it has also its technical, social, and institutional aspect in the long run.

If the share of public investment needed to offset the widening gap steadily increases, will not this bring about a complete structural change as envisaged by Marx, the collectivization of the means of production on an ever larger scale?

How much public control will be needed for the maintenance of full employment in the later stages? How will permanent full employment affect the relation between capital and labor? How will it affect the price and wage structure? What will be its impact on the balance of trade and the balance of payments? These are only a few questions among many others that call for treatment from the long-period aspect.

The vastness, complexity, and extreme dynamism of full employment is not presented in the Keynesian system, nor are its full implications in social and structural terms in the long run. It is perhaps here that we find the greatest contrast between Marx's and Keynes's treatment. The long-term analysis in the Keynesian system is still to be elaborated. It is long overdue and badly needed.

John Law and John Maynard Keynes

The parallel between John Law of Lawriston (1671–1729), controller-general of French finance, a Scottish gentleman descended from an ancient Edinburgh family, and John Maynard Keynes (1883–1946) goes so deep and covers so wide a ground, even touching some aspects of their personal life, that a spiritualist might say that Keynes was a reincarnation of Law after two centuries.

Both were early remarkable for their proficiency in mathematics. Mr. Budgell, a contemporary of Law, writes of him: "His talents and genius lay particularly in Figures," while Keynes also had a mathematical mind, winning a scholarship to King's College, Cambridge, in mathematics and classics, and becoming twelfth wrangler in the mathematical tripos. He published a remarkable work of mathematical philosophy, the *Treatise on Probability* (1921).

Both had many interests, and were masters of a variety of other subjects apart from their main specialty. In *A Full and Impartial Account of the Company of Mississippi,* published in 1721, we read of Law: "Has not the world always said of him 'that he had a superior Genius, and fit for every thing'? Besides the Arts and Sciences, to which he all his life devoted himself, he is a perfect master of Accounts." The rôle of Lord Keynes as a promoter of the arts, theater, music, and ballet is very well known. He organized the Camargo Ballet, built and opened the Arts Theatre in Cambridge, and became Chairman of the Arts Council in 1945.

Both had a charming personality, of "polished and agreeable manners and of much conventional talents."[25] A contemporary of

---

[25] *Dictionary of National Biography.*

Law already mentioned described him thus: "His Person and Address were graceful and easy, his way of thinking strong and nervous, he spoke our tongue perfectly well, and is said to have had a peculiar Happiness in conveying his own Notions in their full strength to those with whom he conversed."[26] And in the obituary of Lord Keynes in *The* (London) *Times*[27] we find a similar description of Keynes as "radiant, brilliant, effervescent, gay, full of impish jokes. His entry into the room invariably raised the spirits of the company. . . . The brilliant wit, the wisdom and the range of his private conversation . . . would have made him a valued member of any intellectual salon or coterie in the great ages of polished discussion."

The same contemporary of Law quoted above describes him as "the Author of the greatest and most surprising Events," one of those persons who "naturally draw the Eyes and Attention of Mankind upon them." Lord Keynes was not so widely famous as was Law in his time, but he attained the greatest fame among the economists of his day, having a world-wide influence both on thought and action.

Both were men of action as well as of thought, and both were active in the same fields. Both made concrete proposals for tax reforms, Lord Keynes proposing a scheme for deferred credits in the pamphlet *How to Pay for the War* (1940). Both took an active part in finance and banking, Law as the founder of great banks and trading companies, Keynes as a member of the Royal Commission on Indian Currency and Finance, a member of the Macmillan Committee on Finance and Industry, and a director of the Bank of England, being nominated, two months before his death, first Governor of the International Monetary Fund and of the International Bank for Reconstruction and Development.

---

[26] *Letter of MacLaw upon his Arrival in Great Britain,* 1721.
[27] *The Times,* April 22, 1946.

Both advocated bold and unorthodox methods in banking. Both had the same craving for adventure, although in its second incarnation, Keynes, this spirit of adventure proceeded more cautiously, after having met with a disastrous failure in a fantastic career during its first incarnation, Law.

Both Law and Keynes were sworn enemies of a gold currency, or the gold standard, and both advocated a managed paper currency, Law in internal, Keynes in international, economy. Law presented his plan of paper money backed by land-values, while Keynes presented the so-called Keynes's plan of "bancor" backed by the flow of trade and the international store of raw materials.

Both were regarded as defenders of state socialism, Law as its precursor, Keynes as a man who presented a new version of it in his conception of socialization of investment. Both were very original thinkers who shocked their respective generations. Both were fond of writing letters, notes, and memoranda, in which much valuable material is found. Finally, both died prematurely, in effect from exceptionally heavy and prolonged strain, Law at 58, Keynes at 63.

Are you serious in suggesting, the astonished reader may ask, that Keynes was the John Law of the twentieth century? I do not know, but on reading Law after Keynes it struck me that there is here a case of a perfect renewal on a higher level of the same doctrine, not only in its major features but also in smaller details.

Let us now consider the similarities, or in many points the identity, of their two doctrines as expounded in their writings. Both present a unique mixture of mercantilism, socialism, and liberalism, more or less the same in its composition. Keynes is neomercantilist, neoliberal, and neosocialist. Why neomercantilist? Because he defends the active balance of trade, regarding it as foreign investment which provides employment and a multiplication of income (foreign trade multiplier). Law holds exactly the same view. Even the idea of the foreign trade multiplier is expounded in Law's writings. In his *Proposals and Reasons for Constituting a Council of Trade in Scotland,* published about 1700, he writes:

". . . Nationally speaking, and all things considered, every penny gotten by the Kingdom in foreign trade, may justly be reckoned worth three by any other home improvement: and that commonly where any particular man gets a penny, the nation in general may get seven or eight; since besides the influence the increase of our foreign trade must needs have on all our home industry. . . ."

This is exactly the idea of a foreign trade multiplier and a multiplier in general presented *in nuce.* Apart from the original increase we have to reckon also the derivative, the secondary increase of employment and income by reason of the influence on home trade. But neither Law nor Keynes is in favor of mere restrictions and controls. Rather both are at heart liberals with qualifications.

Keynes, in advocating his scheme for socialization of investment through control of the flow of money, says that he wanted to save the system of free enterprise, not to destroy it. What is wrong is the quantitative aspect of capitalism, the failure to employ all hands. And Law develops more or less the same views. When he advocates his cheap money policy, he says, "but not by restraints"; when he advocates full employment and relief of the poor, he adds, but "not by charity"; when he advocates the active balance of trade, he stipulates, "not by tariffs" but by full employment.

What of their socialism? Keynes is what we may call an investment, money, and credit socialist, but can we say the same of Law? The likeness between Marx and Keynes is very well known, and I speak of it in another chapter. But in what sense can we speak of Law's socialism?

Many basic theses of socialism are contained in Law's doctrine, and Law's ideas were popular at the time of the great Revolution in 1789, which drew heavily on his ideas, just as the socialists of 1848 drew on those of Louis Blanc and Proudhon.

The great socialist Louis Blanc writes of Law that he wanted to create "une banque qui aurait pour mission de vérifier les promesses de l'homme pauvre. . . ."; that his idea was "permettre au cultivateur de reprendre courage, au pauvre de respirer."[28] The French socialists of 1848 regarded Law as a forerunner of socialism, as a socialist, according to Alphonse Jobet, writing against Law in 1848 in *Une Préface au Socialisme ou le système de Law et la chasse aux Capitaliste.* There is undoubtedly a socialist undertone in Law's writings.

Law writes in his *Proposals* in 1700: "In matters of trade, the interest of particular men and that of their country is so far from being always the same, that they are ofttimes directly opposite to one another, 'tis the true interest of a country that the many should rather get every one a little, than a few should get much, because the more diffusive and universal the gain, the more it will naturally contribute to the growth and progress of industry; whereas on the contrary, the more 'tis limited and restrained, the more it tends to the clogging and cramping thereof. . . ."

Keynes could subscribe to this statement. His whole theory of saving and consumption is an elaboration of this theme. By concentration of wealth the propensity to save is increased, with harmful effects.

Again and again in all Law's proposals there is one constantly recurring refrain: the employment and relief of the poor, based rather on economic reasons of maximization of national output ("our yearly value") than on humanitarian reasons. We read again in the *Proposals*:

". . . in all societies, whether great or small, those who bear rule,

---

[28] *Histoire de la Révolution française,* VI, pp. 278–280.

are highly obliged, and deeply concerned, both in justice and interest to provide convenient and sufficient work, and subsistence for those committed to their care . . ." and Law went on to say that if his monetary proposals for full employment were accepted, then ". . . these people who are now the greatest burthen to the industry of the Kingdom may be made its principal support: and those who are now the great and principal means of our poverty, may become the chiefest cause of our wealth, for these are the hands that must put all that we have before spoken of in motion, and it is only in proportion to their number of capacities, that things can be undertaken and done, and therefore as before this constitution be introduced, it might properly enough be said, we have too many people, yet then we shall be found to have too few." Law rightly foresaw the scarcity of manpower in a fully employed economy.

In his advocacy of full employment Law uses the same opportunity-cost principle applied to the society as a whole as does Keynes. Even if the employer actually incurs a loss for his firm, the society as a whole may gain, because for society it is the national income that counts, not the net income of the employer. Law's reasoning in this regard is much superior to that of Ricardo, who saw only profit, rent, and interest as the net income of the community.

In his *Money and Trade Considered* (Edinburgh, 1705) Law writes as follows:

"An addition to the Money adds to the value of the Country. So long as Money gives Interest, it is imployed; and Money imployed brings Profite, tho' the Imployer loses. If 50 Men are set to Work, to whom 25 Shillings is payed per day, and the Improvement made by their Labour be only equal to, or worth 15 sh. Yet by so much the Value of the Country is increased. But as it is reasonable to suppose their Labour equal to 40 sh. So much is added to the value of the Country, of which the Imployer gains 15 sh. 15 may be supposed to equal the Consumption of the Labourers, who before lived on Charity, and 10 sh. remains to them over their Consumption" (Chap. II).

And in another connection:

"A Nation may gain where the Merchant loses, but wherever the Merchant gains, the Nation gains equal, and so much more, as the Maintenance and Wages of the People employed and the Duty on the Goods amounts to.

"As Trade depends on Money, so the encrease or decrease of the People depends on Trade. If they have Employment at Home, they are kept at Home: And if the Trade is greater then serves to Employ the People, it brings more from places where they are not Employed. Sir William Petty values a Man at 20 years Purchase, by that Computation a Seaman whose wages is 40 shil. a Month, is valued 480 Lib."

Now let us consider some of Law's specific suggestions. His program, set forth in 1700 in the *Proposals,* consists of seven points and contains *inter alia* the following demands:

"1. The imploying and relieving the poor, and the repressing of idleness and sloth,

"2. The reducing the interest of money to three per cent per annum or less, not by force or restraint, but by easy and effectual means.

"3. The effectual carrying on, countenancing, protecting and supporting the foreign trade.

"4. Erecting of national granarys and stores of corn, so as that the industry of this Kingdom may not as hitherto be at any time clogged by extream cheapness, now crusht by the extream dearth of grain."

The three other proposals advocate the undertaking of great physical investments.

93

The strange thing about this program is that all the points, including the plea for national granaries and stores and physical investment, were actually advocated by Keynes. They are not only in accordance with the spirit of his doctrine, but with its letter. It is very interesting to read the arguments by which Law advocated a cheap money policy. He argues with his adversaries in a way similar to that in which Dr. Dalton, Keynes's disciple, when Chancellor of the Exchequer in the British Labour Government, argued with the members of the Opposition.

"It may be objected . . . that this lowering of interest, may not only be a prejudice to them, but to several widows, orphans and other weak people, who live only, or for the most part on their money; but to this it may be answered, that . . . they are not one in two hundred to the rest of mankind; and how unaccountable would it be for a country, either to make or keep up laws to encourage and indulge one in two hundred of their people, not only to live idle themselves, but by the influence of their usurys and extortion as well as example, to crush the industry of others. . . . Besides all this it ought to be considered that by fall of the interest, the ways of gaining, would be so multiplyed, and such comfortable and creditable methods for maintenance and supports would of course be provided for such as really could not live or subsist of themselves, as would be much more than capable of compensating the real loss of any, who in such a case could in the least deserve the public care or commiseration." (Here we have also the germ of Kaldor-Hick's idea of measuring the effects of social welfare policy by the test of whether the loss of those people who are adversely affected by any measure could be compensated by the gain of those people who are better off as a result of the same measure.)

And Law recapitulates his policy of cheap money by adding a new argument:

"It is only by our home industry that we can be best enabled to raise ships, vessels, materials for navigation and proper commodities for foreign vent," and this will be facilitated by "the due and orderly imployment of the poor, the moderate and regular rates of corn and other provisions," as also of "materials for manufacture and interest of money."

We see the same zeal in protesting against the original sin of deflation in both Law and Keynes. Law writes in this connection in his *Proposals*:

"There is no doubt but extream plenty and cheapness contribute exceedingly to extream dearth and want, and that like other extremities, they produce one another; it was observed, that for several years, before the last five, corn was extream cheap and low even so as to discourage both the raiser and heretor, and to indulge the poor in idleness and sloth contracted by plenty . . . was doubtless none of the least causes of the late grievous famine."

In one of his many letters Law writes:

"La banque est, par rapport aux finances, le coeur du royaume, où tout l'argent doit revenir pour recommencer la circulation. Ceux qui veulent l'amasser et le retenir sont comme des parties ou des extrémités du corps humain qui voudraient arrêter au passage le sang qui les arrose et qui les nourrit; elles détruiraient bientôt le principe de la vie dans le coeur, dans toutes les autres parties du corps et enfin dans elles-mêmes."

("The bank is, in respect to finance, the heart of the realm, where all money should return to recommence circulation. Those who wish to hoard and keep it are like parts or extremities of the body that should desire to check the flow of the blood that irrigates and nourishes them; soon they would destroy the life force in the heart, in all the other parts of the body, and finally in themselves.")

It was Keynes's idea also that the circulation of money and credit is the heart of national economy, and that the whole planning can be performed by manipulating and controlling money and credit. And all those who want to secure themselves by their excessive propensity to save harm and upset the national economy, finally destroying themselves.

Law always advocated balancing the budget, not by more taxation, but by a general increase of national income, or what he calls the "yearly value" of the country. He believed that the adoption of his scheme of a cheap money policy should make it possible to take off several taxes. In the *Full and Impartial Account of the Company of Mississippi,* he boasted that "the Regent has taken off several taxes in Paris and the Provinces; so that all France partakes of the Advantages of his happy Administration." This view of the budget was always that of Lord Keynes as well.

We thus see the truely astonishing range of similarities, which may better be called identity of views qualified only by differences of time and the progress of economic analysis, between Law and Keynes. The reason for this similarity is to a great extent the recurrence of the same historic experience: catastrophic unemployment, especially in Scotland and France, the ruin of the nobility in Law's time and of English industry in Keynes's in the interwar period, the disastrous fall of prices and too strict adherence to the rules of a specie currency wholly inadequate to the needs of expanding trade. In his *Letter to Mr. Law upon His Arrival in Great Britain,* Budgell, already quoted, writes: "You will find our Trade lost, our Credit ruined, our Money in the Hands of the basest Men among us, and the Innocent and Deluded still groaning under the Oppression of the Wicked and the Insatiable."

But the strangest thing is that Keynes never quoted Law, not even in the "Note on Mercantilism" in his *General Theory,* where he cites Mandeville and many other minor writers, including so-called "cranks."

The East India Company and the Rise of British Liberalism

Perhaps the clearest and most interesting example of strict relation between a doctrine and powerful interests was the part played by the East India Company in the rise of British economic liberalism. Of course the rise of British liberalism has various sources, being the outcome of many strictly interrelated factors which form the changing historical pattern of life, and this problem has been analyzed by many writers. The economists tend to a purely logical and ideological analysis, while the historians concentrate more on the political or social aspect of the problem. Without contesting that all those aspects are relevant and important, let us try here to concentrate solely on the influence exercised by the powerful group of interests which constituted the East India Company. I am not contending that this influence was the most potent factor in the rise of British liberalism, but I am sure that the rôle of the Company in the development of British liberal economic thought would be a most exciting and fruitful subject for a deep, searching historical study. My treatment here, however, is confined merely to setting up signposts to such a study.

The East India Company had to defend itself as an exporter of bullion and as an importer of silk and spices and of precious cargoes, mostly luxuries of the time, not only against the criticism of nationalists and crude mercantilists, but first of all against the Turkey Company and the opposition of home industry. India herself absorbed enormous quantities of the precious metals, which disappeared into hoards without any trace, as is basically true of India up to the present time. But the Company brought back from India riches, jewels, silk, spices, and above all cheap printed cottons and calicoes, which competed with home woolens and silks, and reexported them at a great profit to other countries. How great were the profits of the world's biggest Company can be shown from its huge dividends, which in the first years of its existence reached 100 per cent, and later, when the principle of self-investment was adopted, varied from 6 to 12½ per cent. The Company maintained its private armies and navies (by 1735 it had seven large warships and many smaller vessels) with their stations and fortifications; had its own merchant navy; conducted wars with French companies; administered huge foreign territories; exercised legislative and judicial powers; possessed its own educational establishments, including later on its own college; had its forts, settlements, docks, and depots; granted loans and gifts to the Treasury; and produced also its array of political and economic writers.

The English weavers and spinners asked for protection from this competition, and obtained it through a series of Calico Acts, the last of which in 1721 prohibited the use or sale of printed, flowered, or dyed calico in England. (The English cotton manufacturers who imitated Indian cotton goods obtained exemption fourteen years later from these prohibitions.) The controversy over protection *v.* freedom of trade raged throughout almost the whole century with varying success. The East India trade not only revolutionized the English textile industry, thus paving the way for the Industrial Revolution, but also revolutionized the economic ideas of the age by battering constantly at the cruder forms of balance-of-trade arguments. It provided all the theoretical weapons afterwards used so splendidly by Adam Smith, being melted down into a new and refined, consistent and sweeping theory. The main arguments of the economic liberalism of the late seventeenth and early eighteenth century were freely supplied, vigorously defended, and highly developed by the the managers, officials, and writers of and for the East India Company. These arguments were deeply rooted in the Company's vested interests, which, however, proved to be the interest of the growth, development, and prosperity of the whole country.

But the great historians of the seventeenth and eighteenth centuries, who record only impersonal ideas and theories without bothering about the deeper personal motives of writers who defended and expounded them, very often have great difficulty in describing and grasping the true ideological atmosphere and the theoretical conception of the epoch. Eli F. Heckscher, the historian of the age of mercantilism, writes: "This is not to deny that advanced *laissez-faire* arguments also occurred here and there even before the end of the 17th century, and this, indeed, even in authors who in other respects were purely mercantilists. And this is not unnatural . . . [here follows a most involved explanation of this phenomenon on a purely logical ground] . . . for however clearly it could be shown that social causation and state interference could go together, it was still but a small step from the conception of an existing social causal interdependence and a mastery over nature in social matters to the conception that such interdependence had an inherent rationality which ought not be disturbed. The general dominance of the idea of natural right was calculated to add fuel to such arguments."[29]

Not the "dominance of the idea" added fuel to the *laissez-faire* ideas, but the dominance of the East India Company, whose shares were owned by most eminent personalities including the Court. And the advanced *laissez-faire* arguments occurred not here and there, but in a great stream. If, however, they occurred "in authors who in other respects were purely mercantilists," it was because most writers who professed them defended quite openly the interests of the East India Company, which were partly based on ex-

---

[29] Eli F. Heckscher; *Mercantilism*, tr. from the German by Mendel Shapiro. London: Allen and Unwin, Ltd., 1935. (First published in Sweden in 1931.)

clusive mercantilistic privileges and partly on a free trade, i.e., anti-protectionist, antibullionist and antistate interference policy.

Thomas Mun (1571-1641), author of *A Discourse of Trade* (1621) and *England's Treasure by Forraign Trade* (1630) was a director of the East India Company. Josiah Child (1630-1699), author of the *Discourse of Trade* (final edition, 1690) was director and later Governor of the East India Company. And both, as is well known, expounded the most enlightened and progressive ideas, on which the liberal economists drew freely a hundred years later.

The whole weight of Mun's treatise lies really in Chapter IV of *England's Treasure,* which states briefly, to quote the title, that "The exportation of our Moneys in Trade of Merchandize is a means to increase our Treasure." Mun gives as illustration of this thesis the East India trade, contending "this profit will be far greater when wee trade in remote Countreys, as for example, if wee send one hundred pounds into the East Indies to buy Pepper there, and bring it hither, and from hence send it for Italy or Turkey, it must yield seven hundred thousand pounds at least in those places, in regard to excessive charge which the Marchant disburseth in those long voyages in Shipping, Wages, Victuals, Insurance, Interest, Customes, Imports and the like, all which notwithstanding the King and the Kingdom gets." He generalizes his thesis into a theory which turns against the Merchant Adventurers' Company, Turkey Company, and many other rivals, and which reads as follows: "Where the voyages are short and the wares rich, which therefore will not employ much Shipping, the profit [i.e., for the country] will be far less." This theory has a quite clear meaning.

Sir Josiah Child, in his book, defends the interests of his Company, showing that it:

1. "Constantly employs twenty five to thirty Sail of the most

Warlike Ships in England with Sixty to a Hundred Men in each ship.

2. "Supplies the Nation constantly and fully with that (in this Age) necessary material of Salt-Petre.

3. "Employs the Nation for its Consumption with Pepper, Indico, Calicoes and several useful Drugs.

4. "Furnishes us with Pepper, Cowryes, Long-Cloth and other Calicoes and painted Stuffs, proper for the Trade of Turkey, Italy, Spain, France and Guiny . . . and these Goods exported to produce in foreign parts, to be returned to England, six times the Treasure in Specie, that the Company exports from hence."

Or take Charles Davenant, who writes his *Essay on the East India Trade* (1696) in the form of a letter to the Marquis of Normanby, who had asked him for an opinion on this matter. In this Essay he has "endeavour'd to show . . . first, that this trade is beneficial to the Kingdom, secondly that 'tis not prejudicial to the General Wollen Manufacture of England, thirdly that it does not so interfere with our Silk and Linnen Manufactures, as to hurt the Publick, fourthly, that the intended Prohibitions may probably occasion an utter Loss of the whole Traffic." The whole work is so conceived that there is no doubt that the whole tract was written for the benefit of the East India Company, if not to its order. Again, Davenant writes on the same subject in a more detailed way, arguing with Pollexfen in his *Discourses on the Public Revenues and the Trade of England.* His basic idea, which could be subscribed to by Adam Smith, is contained in the following excerpt:

"Gold and silver are indeed the measure of trade, but the spring and original of it in all nations, is the natural or artificial product of the country; that is to say, what their land, or what their labour and industry produces. And this is so true that a nation may be supposed by some accident, quite without the species of money, and yet, if the people are numerous, industrous, versed in traffic, skilled in sea affairs, and if they have good ports, and a soil fertile in variety of commodties, such a people will have trade and gather wealth, and they shall quickly get among them a plenty of gold and silver; so that the real and effective riches of a country is its native product."[30]

"Money is at bottom no more than the counters, with which men in their dealings, have been accustomed to reckon . . . this natural or artificial product being most of it the result of the people's labour and industry. . . ."

Davenant also proposes a "scheme for setting the Poor to work," urging, a hundred years before Malthus, that "all the laws made for the provision of the poor, and for punishing idle vagrant persons, be repealed. . . ." In his *Reflections upon the Constitution and Management of the African Trade,* he upholds the Royal African Company's claim for the "exclusive privileges in trade with Africa" with twelve far-fetched and very doubtful arguments, among which is the argument that the natives, "a very cunning as well as deceitful people, never missed catching hold of the advantages which they saw naturally arising to themselves from our separate interests, as well as different methods of management," by "raising the price of negroes, gold, elephant teeth" and by "beating down the value of all woolen and other British manufactures." The competing merchants sell the Negroes at exorbitant prices to the planters, who in turn raise the price of sugar and other colonial articles. There is no doubt that the whole tract was written for the benefit and to the order of the Company in a subservient way.

Another staunch defender of *laissez-faire* principles is Edward Misselden (1608–1654), author of *Free Trade, or the meanes To Make Trade Flourish* and the *Circle of Commerce* (1623). He was deputy-governor of the Merchant Adventurers' Company at Delft

---

[30] Charles Davenant: *Discourses on the Public Revenues and the Trade of England.* Discourse I.

for ten years and was also employed by the East India Company, for which he acted as a Commissioner at Amsterdam in the treaty negotiations with the Dutch. In his first discourse he defends his own Company, but he also has warm words to say about the East India Company. "This Great and Noble Societie . . ." is ". . . far beyond any other Company of this Kingdom." He strives hard to reconcile the principle of exclusive trade privileges, which he calls the principle of "Government and order in Trade," with the defense of free trade. ". . . The name and nature of Monopoly, is more talk't of, then well understood of many; and some thinke that the reducing of trade into Order and Government, is a kinde of Monopolizing and restraint of trade. . . ."[31]

His second treatise, the *Circle of Commerce,* is a polemic against Malynes' defense of the home woolen market. He tries to show that the roots of the bad economic conditions lie not in the organization of trade and the conduct of trade companies, but in unemployment, which goes with poverty and luxury or excess.

Now let us look at the anonymous tracts published by and for the East India Company. They make most interesting reading. They are very enlightened economic treatises on the subject of freedom of trade, international division of labor, the real nature and substance of wealth; and they put forward most cogent arguments against the prejudice of the favorable balance of trade, against an over-all protection and the bullionist conception of wealth.

In one of these tracts,[32] printed in 1677, the East India Company says: "This Rule [the active balance of trade] seems to be taken from the consideration of the whole Kingdom as to its Trade with foreign pacts, under the notion of a single person possessing and managing an Estate or Farm. . . . Yet not withstanding, the said

---

[31] Edward Misselden, *Free Trade, or The Meanes to Make Trade Flourish* (1651 edition), p. 54.
[32] *The East India Trade, a Most Profitable Trade to the Kingdom, etc.*

Rule as it is . . . is not an adequate Rule to measure the whole extent of Foreign Trade by; for it supposseth only a Trading in Commodities, and makes Money, i.e. Gold and Silver, to be fixed Stock and Riches of the Kingdom; and not improvable in the Trade, but encreased or diminished, as it supplys only to answer the Balance of the Trade of Commodities. Whereas in Truth the Stock and Riches of the Kingdom, cannot properly be confined to Money, nor ought Gold and Silver to be excluded from being Merchandise, to be Traded with, as well as any other sort of goods.

"It is true that usually the measure of Stock or Riches is accounted by Money; but that is rather in imagination than reality; A man is said to be worth Ten thousand pounds, when possibly he hath not One hundred pounds in ready Money; but his Estate, if he be a Farmer, consists in Land, Corn or Cattel and Husbandry implements: If a Merchant, in Goods and Merchandise at home or Adventures abroad, or in Shipping; in like manner the Stock or Riches of the Kingdom doth not only consist in our Money, but also in our Commodities and Ships for Trade, and in our Ships of War, and Magazines furnished with all necessary Materials. . . .

"It is a great mistake, though a common one, to think that it is the plenty or scarcity of Money that is the cause of a good or a bad Trade; It is true, when the Trade is quick and good, Money is more seen, and changeth hands ten times for what it doth when the Trade is dull and dead, so that One hundred pounds in a time of quick Trading, makes as great an appearance as one Thousand pounds in a time of dead Trading. It is not so much the Money that influenceth the Trade, as it is the Trade that discovers the Money, which otherwise would lie hid. . . ."

It is impossible not to see here the basic textures of Adam Smith's arguments in his *The Wealth of Nations,* written 100 years later. The East India writers who defended their Company against the protectionist arguments of the home industry always started their tracts with a general exposition of the principles of trade and economy. They would say invariably, as modern propagandists do: "Give me leave in the first place to say something of trade in general, which may throw some light on our special problem related to the India trade"; and in doing so they expounded, defended, and enlarged the *laissez-faire* doctrine in economics, much before the independent thinkers and students did, giving the latter material to think and work upon.

Let us take another tract of the East India Company, called a *"Triatise"* with a very long title in five points ("wherein is Demonstrated I. that the East India Trade is the most National of all Foreign Trades, II . . ." and so on through point V), printed at London in 1681. We have here at first the same general observations about the rôle, function, and usefulness of trade in general and foreign trade in particular, and then the defense of liberty of trade and production. It is worth while to record here some of its specific statements:

"All Domestic or Foreign Trade . . . increase(s) the value of our English Lands. . . .

"All Monopolies, of what Nature or kind soever, are Destructive to Trade," even those which (if any) are granted to the East India Company.

"Domestic and Foreign Trade wax and wane together. . . .

"Silver and Gold . . . are no less a Commodity than Wine, Oyl, Tobacco, Cloth or stuffs.

"No Nation ever was or will be considerable in Trade, that prohibits the Exportation of Bullion.

"Whatever Nation hath the lowest Interest, will certainly have their lands in highest esteem and price."

Again the same theme, the same arguments, and the same doctrine of free trade was presented.

There is another small tract of two pages published by the East

India Company anonymously. It has no date, but was most probably written at the same period as the last-mentioned tract. It refutes very thoroughly all the basic arguments of economic policy used by the Company's adversaries—in other companies, small merchants, and weavers and spinners—in the struggle against it. It is called *Remarks on the Complaints Against the Trade to East India as Prejudicial to this Nation*. The main arguments against the Company, says the tract, are based on its action in:

    I. "Carrying out great quantities of Silver,"

    II. "Bringing in large supplies of wrought Silks,"

    III. "Hindring the English Manufacturers and Expence of Wool."

Then comes the refutation of those arguments, with this conclusion:

"It is the interest of England that all its Manufactures be kept up to a due Standard of Goodness, and at such reasonable prices, as our neighbours may not be able to under-work us, but by the Goodness and Cheapness of ours, they may be induced to take them, and be kept from contriving the same or the like sorts of Manufactures."

How is the distress of the woolen industry to be remedied? Only by measures which improve the actual condition of woolen manufacturers, says the tract, for "Restraints and Contrivances to force Trade, as they are rarely found to have the desired success, have generally proved pernicious to our Selves, and to have had evil consequences in being improved against us by our Neighbours."

On the whole, the tract is a very good and reasonable account of a *laissez-faire* doctrine, which embraces all its basic elements, but one, also, which is dictated, with certain exceptions, by self-interest.

*   *   *

It has been said that "ideas have legs." They certainly have, but they also have hearts and pockets. Some writers defend or expound certain ideas because they are at heart in agreement with certain interests; others defend them because they serve as rationalizations of the writers' material interests.

There is a human element in every doctrine, because the writer is not an abstraction but a human being, not only with a brain, but with a heart. Moreover, there are his many institutional and social links to be considered.

A historian who considers only the intellectual or ideological content of a certain doctrine or its finely political aspect sees it in one or two dimensions only; but the world of ideas is three-dimensional. It would be wrong to say that economic doctrines are purely a kind of rationalization of certain interests, whether those of workers, merchants, financiers, industrialists, or farmers, but they are such to a great extent. There is nothing astonishing in that assertion. There is no imputation of hypocrisy to economic writers. Whatever social economic doctrine I profess, be it protectionist, nationalist, liberal, or socialist, in its pure or mixed form, that doctrine, in one way or another, directly or by implication, serves some interests and offends the others. The intellectual or logical side of any doctrine is one thing; its ideological side, which springs rather from the heart than from the head and is linked up with religious, philosophical, and social ideas, is another. The concrete economic business and other material interests in various forms make the third dimension of an economic doctrine.

Is Malthus Still Right?

The pendulum of opinion in population matters swings between two extremes: one emphasizing the danger of overpopulation, the other that of underpopulation. These two opposites are obviously related to two different trends in population movement. Communities with a rapidly growing population and limited resources are disturbed by the imaginary or real perils arising from a population which is becoming too large, while those with a declining rate of growth are disquieted by the menace of their population becoming too small. At present we are inclined to overstate the peril of underpopulation and the benefits connected with a rapid growth. Rapid growth, as has always been affirmed by the American economists since Carey, facilitates transition to mass-production methods, accelerates the progress of technology, and stimulates capital formation through the influence of rising consumption upon investment (the so-called Acceleration Principle). Rapid population growth is the basic outlet for investment.

On the other hand European economists, living in old and overcrowded communities with no openings in new territories, were inclined to follow the more static conception of Malthus that the rapid growth of population has its limitations in natural resources bound up with space, that space is the limiting factor for population growth. The stimulus that comes from a growing population, these economists say, can be replaced by that from rising standards of living. There is no inherent advantage of a rising consumption via increased numbers over that via better standards of nutrition or housing.

Historical experience shows that both contentions are true in different situations, for we can find many examples to illustrate the correlation between the rapid growth of population and progress, and, *vice versa,* that between population growth and decay. The prodigious and unique growth of population in the nineteenth century in Britain, the United States, Germany, and many other countries is typical of the first relation, while India or China today illustrates the second. On the other hand, we also have examples of the correlation of a declining population with progress, or, *vice versa,* with decay and misery. The economic consequences of the Black Death in England may be regarded on the whole as a stimulus to progress, since wage rates increased considerably, agriculture changed over from arable land to pasture, and the liquidation of the medieval system of cultivation was hastened.

In more recent times French prosperity in the nineteenth century was based primarily on the low birth-rate combined with a high propensity to save and invest. But we have also a number of examples in more recent times of a declining population associated with decay, in depressed areas and in poverty-stricken countries where disease and misery go hand in hand.

The truth is that in actual life no one single factor can be made responsible for progress or decay. The growth of population may be a great vehicle of progress if, for instance, technical progress and capital formation really take place, or if this growth coincides with the opening-up of new territories and foreign trade, or if better social and economic institutions supervene. In East Central Europe the growth of population was a vehicle of retrogression, contributing to the misery and undernourishment of men, animals, and plants, to ignorance and disinvestment.

The concept of optimum population is vague and rather ill-defined. Optimum for whom? Since "man is the measure of all things," where are we to find the criterion for optimum population? If it were true that thirty million people living in the British Isles might have a much higher real income per head than forty-seven million, would this mean that thirty million is the optimum population for Great Britain? Or if it were true that fifty-five million people could live in Britain in conditions of fair comfort judged by basic standards of nutrition, housing, and education, would this be the optimum population?

Optimum population means optimum for a given space, the concept itself being derived from biology. Tomatoes, carrots, or peas have a certain optimum space, which varies with the richness of soil, climatic conditions, and the intensity of cultivation. If we fought weeds or insects and parasites more successfully, the optimum space could be in some cases reduced. In this connection the optimum space means optimum for growing a good quality plant, i.e., one with all those potential qualities which we appreciate. Analogously, the optimum population would mean the optimum space required for bringing up good-quality men. But what qualities have we in mind? Here the matter becomes one for philosophers rather than for economists. But even if the answer is agreed on, by analogy with plants we should find that optimum space depends on the extent of natural riches, climatic conditions, the pattern of wants, the stage of technical development, the level of education, the level of capital investment and propensities to save, the pattern of distribution of income and all other institutional arrangements, and, finally, on international relations. By analogy with plants, if we fought more successfully disease, criminality, or social parasitism in our midst, the optimum space could be reduced.

We can ask from a static standpoint what the optimum population would be if all other things remained unaltered, but there is little sense in this question, since with change in the population, almost everything else changes too. Changes in numbers of the population are accompanied by changes in its composition, in the amount and composition of manpower, in the propensity to consume different commodities and services, in the propensity to save and the inducement to invest, and by changes in the division of labor and general productivity. Since man is the measure of all things, everything else changes with man.

But does this mean that Malthus' ideas have lost their meaning for the present generation and belong to the waste material of history? Not at all. In the second edition of the *Essay on the Principle of Population* (1803), Malthus formulated his basic propositions so widely that they can still be accepted as valid—

valid, as a matter of fact, for all times and for all nations. And this is really their weakness.

Let us quote here the two basic propositions of Malthus, which read as follows:

1. "Population invariably increases where the means of subsistence increase, unless prevented by some very powerful and obvious checks."

2. "These checks, and the checks which repress the superior power of population, and keep its effects on a level with the means of subsistence, are all resolvable into moral restraint, vice, and misery."

These propositions are still valid, with only the slight amendment that, for moral restraint, we may read birth-control, and to the positive checks we may add ignorance, since ignorance is as great a factor in mortality as vice and misery.

Nations as well as social strata can be divided into two large classes:

1. Low-income countries or strata, in which the positive checks (vice, misery, and ignorance) still operate fairly strongly, while birth-control plays only a minor part. To this class belong such countries as India, China, and most of the East European countries, apart from colonial or semicolonial countries.

2. High-income countries or strata, in which birth-control is the main check, while positive checks in peacetime play a minor rôle (wars and civil strife are placed among the positive checks). To this class belong all high-income countries, such as Britain and the United States and the countries of Western Europe. But even in high-income countries, positive checks are still in operation, as can be seen from the differential rates of mortality, especially in regard to children.

We can formulate a general proposition that wherever positive checks are in decline, preventive checks seem to grow stronger.

They are never in operation simultaneously in similar strength. The positive checks operate in low-income groups or countries; the preventive checks mainly in high-income groups or countries. Therefore the level and the distribution of income will primarily determine the distribution of positive and preventive checks in their numerical strength. And this fact seems to confirm Sismondi's and Karl Marx's thesis that every economic system has its own law of population—i.e., that every economic system has its own pattern of distribution of positive and preventive checks based on the level and distribution of income and the whole pattern of culture linked with the economic life. Both kinds of checks are mutually interdependent, both are dependent on the level and distribution of income, and, finally, the preventive checks determined by motives are linked with the whole sphere of social and economic motives.

The "law of overpopulation" described by Malthus in the first edition of his *Essay on the Principle of Population* was the law of early capitalism, and is still valid for such countries as India and China, which could profit greatly by following Malthus' advice. The early capitalist development went hand in hand with the free expansion of manpower and markets. The factory system in the early nineteenth century, with its great opportunities for child labor, gave encouragement to high fertility rates and at the same time to the full working of positive checks.

The population trends in latter-day capitalism are being quite reversed, so that they can be brought under the name of the law of underpopulation. We see the slowing down of the annual increase of the population with a simultaneous ageing caused by the increase of natality, which is only partly offset by the decrease of mortality. The preventive checks are operating on such a scale that they seem after a certain time to endanger the survival of a nation. They are no longer fully offset by the decline of the positive checks. High-income countries and strata are in constant ebb, with far-reaching effects for the future pattern of civilization.

The economists in their abstract treatises very often confuse the position of low-income countries with that of a full, mature industrial economy. But there is a world of difference between them, not only in matters of population but in all other basic issues, such as the problem of saving and investment, distribution of income, and degrees and ways of planning. There is a different economic problem for the two categories which justifies different sets of economic propositions.

III

THE FOUR STAGES OF THE DEVELOP-
MENT OF ECONOMIC DOCTRINES

The Dialectical Movement

It is worth while to review the history of economic thought from a distant point, just as we review large stretches of landscape from a high mountain top or from a high-flying aircraft. We then see, not the small details, but rather a kind of plastic map with main curves, contours, and belts. If we investigate the history of doctrines close at hand, we get an amazing and confusing wealth of details and peculiarities, a real turmoil and tumult of ideas where everything is contradicted by everything else, is circumscribed and disallowed. But if we climb higher and take a general view of a large span, in our case of one or more centuries, we get a clearer and more consistent picture of distinctive phases of a doctrinal development. In that case, of course, we have to be highly selective and to pick out only those doctrines and writers who gave the tone to a given epoch, expounding ideas by which an age lived and worked, which were ruling in the sense of being the accepted scale of values. Those doctrines inspired the country's economic policy, its institutions and organization.

The fact of selection, of course, gives our work an air of premeditation. We have an idea beforehand and we select our facts in a way designed to give the idea force by additional arguments which are pseudo-scientific and not historical. Probably the same argument could be used against our visual selection of lines and curves seen from an aircraft. All that we see and think is deeply rooted in our memories and human values; therefore, a mind intellectually untrained and new to history would perhaps present a more objective picture than an economist or historian, as the man blind from birth who suddenly gained his sight in the air would present a more objective picture than the man who has already formed a picture before he goes up in an aircraft.

Still it seems basically true that, looking at the long stretches of the ruling economic teachings from a high plane, we see four basic doctrines which are not economic only, but are also political and social, and in a way philosophical, corresponding fundamentally to four distinct phases of economic, social, and political development and to the development of whole styles of life.

If we review the doctrines that have ruled since the Middle Ages in Western Europe, we find four distinct phases in the development of economic thought: the medieval doctrine of the Schoolmen, corresponding to the feudal and corporate society and to the town economy; the mercantilist doctrine, corresponding to the mercantile system of the absolute and the new territorial national state; the liberal classical or neoclassical doctrine, corresponding to liberal democracy based on world trade; and the socialist doctrine, which corresponds to the ever growing importance of the principle of national planning in its multifarious though not wholly disparate forms.

This development of economic thought is seen most clearly in England, because the transition from mercantilist to liberal and now to the new social economics in thought and policy is here most clearly marked. In other countries liberal thought was interrupted and deformed by the intrusion of nationalistic thought and neomercantilist practice, and in the latest period by full-scale planning for power politics.

Another feature which hardly can be disputed is the dialectical movement in the development of economic ideas and institutions. Indeed the dialectical movement is most clearly seen in the development of economic thought. The coming doctrine is in violent opposition to the doctrine it is to replace in all its basic ideas. The mercantilist school was in violent antagonism to medieval thought; similarly, Adam Smith devotes one-fourth of his book to refuting the "erroneous speculations" of mercantilist political economy. And the school of today starts once more with very violent, and admittedly sometimes unjustified, criticism of the *laissez-faire* doctrine.

We may contend generally that every ruling doctrine of a given age can best be understood in the light of its predecessor. As long as it holds the reins, it has the air of an absolute which has a permanent value for all generations to come, and all else is regarded as ignorance or error. But when its time comes to pass away, its true nature is better revealed by its limitations, which are linked with its assumptions rooted in a given historical context. Therefore every doctrine is really better understood in historical perspective then in its own times. There is nowhere to be found more orthodoxy than among economists. They often swear that the ruling doctrine is the only permanently valid doctrine, applicable to all ages, the only one true to reason and nature. Still they too are gnawed by the tooth of time and constantly yield ground.

Probably this dialectical movement has something to do with the process of constant disillusionment which is going on both on the institutional and psychological plane in addition to constant changes of technique and situation. The institutions wear out, and what we received and experienced also loses its attraction, becoming stale and boring; we want to experience something new. The attraction of novelty plays a great part in the development of both institutions and ideas, but an even greater one, perhaps, in the realm of ideas than in that of institutions. We have to remember that there are some basic values difficult to combine or to keep in their right proportion, such as security and progress, or freedom and equality, or welfare and leisure, so that in the phase following that in which one of the pair is dominant, we are attracted by its opposite. This dialectical movement is a matter of speculation for philosophical and historical minds, presenting an opportunity for a wealth of interpretation, technical, institutional, psychological, and social; but the fact itself cannot be disputed.

Let us now cursorily survey the basic working ideas and concepts of these four stages of economic thought, ideas by which people lived and worked in ages when they were respectively dominant.

The Medieval Doctrine

The first socio-economic doctrine which governed the Western world for nearly four centuries is the scholastic one, best embodied in the teaching of St. Thomas Aquinas. His concept of "distributive justice" (*iustitia distributiva*), as applied to the relations of persons with one another and based on "geometrical equality" which distributes goods and rewards according to rank, merits and birth, is the best expression of the feudal institutions. Every estate has its own rights and duties. Arithmetical equality between men of differing rank and merits would be the greatest injustice. *Suum cuique* is the motto of the traditional society. Aquinas' conception of a society as an organic moral body which comes before the individual and is bound to strict allocation of different functions and tasks, the idea of holism, is the best expression of the ordered society of his time.

The idea of moderation which permeates all the socio-economic structure dominated not by the "economic man" but by the man desirous of maintaining his traditional standard of living according to the estate in which he was born is put forth. The "lust for profit" (*cupiditas lucri*) is condemned. The endless drive for money (*terminum nescit sed in infinitum tendit*)[1] is the main source of social and moral evil. It is not maximum production which counts. *Augere pecuniam in infinitum* is a sinful action. Production should have certain limits in the needs and wants of family life. Economic activity has its proper limits (*mensura debita*) in the traditional standard of living proper to each estate (*ad domus suae sustentationem*).

Work is not only an economic activity, but has many noneconomic, moral, and religious values. It is a duty towards the family (*ad victum quaerendum*), towards the society (*officium*), towards one's own salvation and moral well-being (*ad tollendum otium ex quo multa mala oriuntur*). It is also a form of prayer; therefore its artistic perfection is of great importance.

Since the profit motive is rejected, as well as the drive towards maximum output, there is no need for free competition, but rather for arrangements which support the limitations on economic activity, for rules and regulations which ensure the right relations of persons, their quality of performance, and their right behavior.

The supreme rules are embodied in the conception of justice in exchange (*iustitia commutativa*) based on arithmetical equality, on strict objective equivalence of value (*quod in iustitia commutativa consideratur principaliter aequalitas rei*). From this conception spring the rules of *iustum pretium,* which should cover the cost incurred and the effort of the craftsman or the merchant

---

[1] All Latin quotations are from St. Thomas Aquinas, *Summa Theologica.*

(*labores et expensae*) according to his traditional standard of living. And the idea of *iustum salarium,* coming from the same source, states the rule that every laborer has the right to ask a wage sufficient to ensure the sustenance of his family according to the traditional standard of living (*ius naturale habet, quod homo vivat de labore suo*). It is not the minimum standard of living for all strata which is here meant, not the *necessarium vitae* but the *necessarium personae,* which differs according to the stratum to which that person belongs (*secundum conditionem et statum propriae personae et aliarum personarum, quarum cura ei incumbit*).

The rules and regulations are not state rules imposed above, but codes of behavior emanating from self-governing bodies which look upon themselves not only as professional associations but as social and religious organizations. The strict rules of *iustum pretium* must be judged against the background of merchants and craft guilds, with their strongly entrenched monopolistic position, which could be easily exploited unless strict rules of behavior were imposed.

(The ideas of *iustum pretium* and *iustum salarium,* however, are not only rules, but have a theoretical value, explaining *de facto* the settlement of prices and wages in the age in which those ideas were operative as guiding principles of price fixation in guilds and corporations.)

The negative attitude towards profits was expressed in the theory of the barrenness of money and credit. The main function of money is to serve as a medium of exchange (*pecunia principaliter est inventa ad commutationes faciendas*), and as a source of value it is essentially barren (*res quae non fructificat*), being a consumption good, which is destined for expenditure (*cum pecuniae usus, sit illius rei consumptio, ac distractio, iniustum et illicitum est, pro eius usu aliquid accipere*). The use of money therefore is inseparably connected with its consumption (*proprius et principalis pecuniae usus est ipsius consumptio sive distractio*).

Consequently the substance of money and its use cannot be disposed of separately, as can be done in the case of a house, or a piece of ground, of which the substance may be sold separately from its use. While it is possible to rent a house, to lease a plot of land, or to hire out the work of a horse, and still retain the ownership of those commodities, the use of a consumable commodity such as wine or bread cannot be sold separately from its substance; to sell the use apart from the matter would be to sell what does not exist.

It is easy to see that this theory of the sterility of money and credit was related to consumers' credit, which was then used on a large scale and as a rule proved ruinous to the borrower; producers' credit was scarcely known. Exceptions to the theory were made as soon as it came into contact with the phenomenon of producers' credit. Even St. Thomas Aquinas allows the charging of interest in cases where the money is employed, broadly speaking, for productive purposes. These are just the cases that clearly reflect the economic source of the general theory of the sterility of money in the precapitalist epoch.[2]

The theory of the unproductivity of foreign trade, with a negative attitude especially towards exports, was the best expression of a self-sufficing manor economy concerned mainly with abundance and cheapness of supply, in which foreign trade supplied mainly luxuries.

The scholastic school represents the theological and ethical stage

---

[2] *Summa Theologica*, Quaest. 78, Art. 2. Of the seven cases in which the taking of interest is permissible, the following three deserve special attention: A. If the creditor incurred a loss and the debtor obtained an advantage, the former could claim indemnification. B. If the lender entrusted the money to a trader or an artisan, he could demand a share in the profit. C. If the security taken for the loan yields a profit, *e.g.*, a house or a piece of land.

of economic thought, based on one universally recognized code of morality[3] and the rule of the Roman Catholic Church.

The Mercantile System

The next stage is the mercantile system, covering the epoch of economic history and thought which lies between the medieval and the liberal economy (the sixteenth, seventeenth, and most of the eighteenth centuries, in Great Britain). Here the close correlation between ideas and economic life appears in almost perfect form, producing a vast variety of schools.

In Europe we can distinguish five main versions of that prodigious current of mercantilist thought:

1. The Anglo-Dutch schools, tending towards freer forms of production and trade, with emphasis rather on the balance of payments than merely the balance of trade, and addressing itself to merchants and businessmen rather than to kings and princes.

2. The French school, tending towards industrially minded state socialism (Colbertism).

3. The Italian-Spanish schools, with their interests centered around monetary problems and burdened with ecclesiastical thought and medieval tradition.

4. The German schools, with their interests centered around administrative and fiscal questions (*Polizeiwirtschaft* and *Kameralistic*).

In all countries we see three phases of mercantilism: emergence, development, and decline, and those periods in every country are again different for practice and theory. Mercantilist practice continued for a long time after mercantilist theory was moribund.

---

[3] "The application of ethics to economic transactions was rendered possible by the existence of one universally recognised code of morality, and the presence of one universally accepted moral teacher."

After making those reservations, let us proceed to a brief outline of the main features of the great, powerful, and changing stream which we call mercantilism in the realm of ideas.

First of all we see a close union between economics and politics which has never before or since been attained in any other historical stages. In fact we see the domination of economics by politics and it was at this stage that economics receives the name "political economy"—when Montchrétien in 1615 named his *Traité d'économie politique*. The economy is regarded as means to political power. It is not wealth which is sought but power. Montchrétien explains very well his preoccupation with economics when in his study he proceeds with the successive steps in the order of their importance. The state needs an army, an army needs munitions and provisions, it needs to be paid, that means that good tax yields must be secured, and that in turn means that sufficient income must be provided for its inhabitants. The wealth of the country is only a means to power and grandeur of the state.

The mercantilists were all busy devising new means of acquiring and multiplying wealth. They were the planners on a larger or smaller scale. They were full of organizing drive and zest. Here we can see the full contrast to the preceding phase. Unlike the Schoolmen, the mercantilist writers were rationalists, they were firm believers in the power of reason. They did not believe in tradition, in traditional institutions and organizations. The unrest of the great age of the Renaissance and the quest for the great riches which were to be had by adventure, by great overseas trade, by organization and planning find here full expression. One country sees the great riches accumulated by others and wants to get them. Things are moving fast and everyone is unwilling to be outdistanced by the others. The idea of moderation which permeated the whole thinking of the Schoolmen was entirely replaced by its opposite—the quest for riches.

The mercantilists shared with the Schoolmen the conception of organization of production, but the Schoolmen had in mind the traditional corporate organization of small organic entities, while the mercantilists envisaged state organization by new institutions created for the purpose. The state is the center of economic power and control, and its interests and regards should be predominant. The scholastic doctrine centered around the conception of the local government and local autonomy, while the mercantilist doctrine moved along the lines of centralism. It is really the doctrine of absolute monarchy and the newly developed national state.

The medieval doctrine was universal; the mercantilist doctrine was national. The splitting of the Catholic Church into national churches had a full counterpart in economics. Nicolò Machiavelli can be regarded as the best early representative of the whole trend of ideas. This trend was toward a small nationalism, i.e., nationalism on a small scale but with a definite aggressive taint. In a way Voltaire's dictum: "It is clear that one country cannot gain without another losing,"[4] is the motto of the mercantilist writers.

The Schoolmen believed in international harmony and the brotherhood of men; not so the mercantilists, who saw the national conflicts of interest as the background of economics. The scholastic doctrine was general and abstract, based on deduction from a few generalities, while the mercantilist doctrine was descriptive and immensely practical. Yet mercantilism was really a kind of generalization on specific policies and institutions. It had few general truths to profess, and its theoretical edifice was poor and insufficient. Its merit consists really in asking questions rather than in answering them. Mercantilist writers were primarily concerned with description and analysis of existing or proposed institutions and with collecting facts. In this period falls the school of "Political

---

[4] In his article "Patrie" in the *Dictionnaire philosophique* (1764).

Arithmetik" in England with its emphasis on statistics and demography.

In contrast to the Schoolmen, who believed in essential sterility and barrenness of money, the mercantilist writers were fascinated by the stream of precious metals and by the great fertilizing effect of money. Money for them was not merely a medium of exchange but the means to full production and full employment, the main source of wealth and power of the state. Shortage of money was regarded as the main cause of poverty, unemployment, and general backwardness. John Law's speculations on money and credit are the best illustration of that current of thought. But this emphasis on money should not be regarded as mere bias and ignorance. It was an expression of a real need for money arising out of the transition from a natural to a money economy and the requirements of young territorial states which were organizing their administration and their armies.

Money can be acquired primarily by the development of foreign trade. Its advantages in the new age were obvious and overwhelming. It brought not only wealth but the organization of new territories, giving scope for full development of maritime power. "England Treasure by Foreign Trade, or the Balance by Foreign Trade is the Rule of Our Treasure" (1664)—this title of Thomas Mun's work best expresses the main preoccupation of the mercantilist writers. The balance of trade is for them the pivot of the whole system, because by an active balance of trade a country increases its stock of money and its productive power. This idea has a nationalistic color and is based on the conviction that the volume of trade is limited, so that when one nation increases its share the shares of other nations are lowered.

The mercantilist writers defend the producers and merchants, not the consumers, as the liberal school later did. They disregard the consumers' interests and identify the interests of producers with that of the country. Spending is regarded as the source of wealth and progress; saving does not find that praise which will be encountered in the writings of the liberal school. More expenditure is said to bring more income; extravagance and luxury are encouraged; and a program of magnificent buildings and public works is continually planned. In a way Mandeville's thesis that a "private vice" may be a "public benefit" expresses the view of the age.

Ideas on population center around encouragement for the growth of population. The danger of overpopulation does not occur to the mercantilist writers in an age when wars, civil disease, and poverty wrought such havoc among the population. To increase the numbers of the population was alleged to increase power and wealth; thus the German mercantilist V. L. von Seckendorff in his work *Der deutsche Fürstenstaat* (1655) writes: "The greatest treasure of the country consists in numbers of well-nourished people," and the saying of another German mercantilist, J. H. G. von Justi (1771), that "a State can never be overpopulated" is well known. A century later this statement was to be regarded as a strange one.

The basic conception of "power through national wealth" was interpreted in a plutocratic way, wealth being taken to mean wealth for the monopolists and for those privileged by charters and exclusive rights. The conception of popular welfare was absent. The wage level, it was thought, must be kept low for the sake of the balance of trade, because this situation would favor competition on the market with other countries. One of the objects of the Poor Laws was to enable manufacturers to employ wage-earners as cheaply as possible, low wages being partially made good by contributions from the parishes.

The second stage in economic doctrine, then, was the political stage, with economics subservient to politics.

The Laissez-Faire Doctrine

The third stage of economic thought covers the period of approximately 150 years which begins with Adam Smith's *The Wealth of Nations* (1776). Its most outstanding early representatives are Adam Smith and David Ricardo. Its central idea is wealth for its own sake as expressed in the rule of maximization of net profit.

The physiocratic idea that only the net product (*produit net*) (from agriculture) counts as a source of the wealth of nations and as a vehicle of progress develops into a similar conception that the source of wealth and progress is net income, including net profits, interest, and rent, while wages serve only for the reproduction of the human agents of production. The best and most frank expression of this idea is to be found in Ricardo's *Principles* (Book 2, Chap. XXVI), which reads as follows:

"Provided its net real income, its rent and profits be the same, it is of no importance whether the nation consists of ten or twelve millions of inhabitants. Its power of supporting fleets and armies, and all species of unproductive labour, must be in proportion to its net, and not in proportion to its gross income. If five millions of men could produce as much food and clothing as was necessary for ten millions, food and clothing for five millions would be the net revenue. Would it be of any advantage to the country, that to produce this same net revenue, seven millions of men should be required, that is to say, that seven millions should be employed to produce food and clothing sufficient for twelve millions? The food and clothing of five millions would enable us neither to add a man to our army and navy, nor to contribute one guinea more in taxes."

The main emphasis was laid on the accumulation of capital by the saving of net profits (interest and rents). Capital is the ruler and the benefactor of society. It brings more employment and higher efficiency, promoting the division of labor and a higher standard of living. The road to prosperity leads therefore through maximum savings of maximum profits. Adam Smith in *The Wealth of Nations* (Book IV, Chap. 2) writes: "The industry of the society can augment only in proportion as its capital augments, and its capital only in proportion to what can be gradually saved out of its revenue." And elsewhere (Book II, Chap. 3): "By what a frugal man annually saves, he not only affords maintenance to an additional number of productive hands, for that or the ensuing year, but, like the founder of a public workshouse, he establishes, as it were, a perpetual fund for the maintenance of an equal number in all times to come. . . . The frugal is the public benefactor."

The economic theory of that age is the theory of profit, saving, and capital. Liberal thought is the doctrine of self-interest which is in providential harmony with the interests of the society. "By preferring the support of domestic to that of foreign industry, he [the enterpreneur] intends only his own security; and by directing that industry in such a manner as its produce may be of the greatest value, he intends only his own gain, and he is in this, as in many other cases, led by an invisible hand to promote an end which was no part of his intention. By pursuing his own interest he frequently promotes that of the society more effectually than when he really intends to promote it." The glorification of self-interest finds its highest expression in Malthus' doctrine, which condemns social services as harmful to the society. To Malthus self-interest is the will of God: "He has enjoined every man to pursue as his primary object his own safety and happiness and the safety and happiness of those immediately connected with him, and it is highly instructive to observe, that in proportion as the sphere contracts and the power of giving effectual assistance increases, the desire increases at the same time. . . . By this wise provision the most ignorant are led to promote the general happiness, an end which they would totally fail to attain if the moving principle of conduct had been benevolence."[5]

Seventy years later, writing in the same climate of thought, Stanley Jevons describes the subject-matter of his work as "the mechanics of utility and self-interest."[6] And the *laissez-faire* doctrine ends in the attempts of the psychological and mathematical school to establish an exact calculus of pleasure and pain for the individual: "Pleasure and pain are undoubtedly the ultimate objects of the Calculus of Economics. . . ." In other words, to "maximise pleasure is the problem of Economics," writes Jevons.

The glorification of natural impulses turns into a glorification of liberty and the belief that liberty is the practical, almost magical, answer to all social problems, however difficult they may be. The physiocrats, and after them the classical school, discovered the existence of a "natural order" (*ordre naturel*) of society governed by an "Invisible Hand" and based on the rights to liberty, self-interest, and property. Restraint, compulsion, or controls are unnatural, being a violation of these natural rights and opposed to the eternal economic laws based on these principles.[7]

The eternal laws of economics are market laws which can be discovered by pure analysis on the basis of some few concepts properly understood and handled. Pure theory of value and prices, pure theory of wages and profits, pure theory of capital and interest are the lines of investigation into the unchanging mechanism of the market economy based on the eternal principles of liberty, self-interest, and property.

Every one of the factors of production receives "the natural rec-

---

[5] *An Essay on the Principle of Population,* seventh edition. London, 1872.

[6] *Theory of Political Economy,* Introduction.

[7] The same line of thought is still defended today in Professor Hayek's *Road to Serfdom* (1944).

ompense," the natural reward due to it according to its contribution to the product. The laws of distribution are not social or institutional or historical laws, they are natural laws similar to the laws of the physical world.

The "Invisible Hand" which rules the economic world is the market mechanism. It keeps demand and supply in equilibrium, and in the long run equilibrates the production and consumption of various goods, ensuring the optimum size of different industries and employments. The governing factor is market price, which is in short-term equilibrium when supply is equal to demand, and in long-term equilibrium when the market price equals cost price (natural price), which is another way of saying that all marginal returns tend to be equal. To discover the position of equilibrium and to formulate the laws of a static and automatic economy was thought to be the main task of economic theory. And economic theory finally turned into a theory of equilibrium in close analogy to a mechanistic conception. Small changes were investigated, and the movements of margins were related to movements of prices and returns on the assumption of optimum satisfaction of consumers and optimum profits of producers, while the greater changes related to income levels were neglected.

The functional, not the structural, side was the object of study, and on the functional side one aspect was in the foreground, the theory of value.

Economics in that age was primarily a theory of value; it was conceived as price-economics. The objects of its study were production and distribution of values, the problems of wages, interest, rents, and profits being treated as the problems of the prices of labor, capital, land, and enterprise; the problem of money and credit as the problem of circulation of values; the problem of the economic cycle as the problem of fluctuation or disturbance in the structure and circuit of values. All problems were stated in relation to price; everything was treated as dependent solely on prices, not on income levels. Thus the theory of value was the foundation-stone of the whole edifice of economics.

It may be said that the economists of that era consciously or unconsciously adopted the attitude of businessmen striving for profits and markets, for the accumulation of capital and wealth by means of free pricing. The objective of businessmen was money-making; this they regarded as the essence of economic life. It is natural that economists should have made the process of money-making through free pricing the main subject of their study. As pricing was the principal weapon in the struggle for profits and markets, the problem of pricing in all its manifold aspects attracted the main attention of students of economics.

The nation as a whole did not participate in this struggle so long as national aims, objectives, and policies could only vaguely be seen and defined. In economic life the individual was presumably the ruler, and all resources were at his command, while group actions, institutions, and aggregates were treated essentially as noneconomic forces, as disturbances of the circuit of values.

It is not surprising that the activities of trade unions, or of state regulations, were treated as a form of political or economic power which deformed the process of natural pricing, and the most striking attitude in this respect may be found in Boehm-Bawerk's study *Control or Economic Law (Macht oder ökonomisches Gesetz)*.[8] The change of structure was not acknowledged; the structural pattern of economic forces was either overlooked or reasoned away as nonexistent or as belonging, not to economics, but to sociology. Collective bodies, groups, institutions of national economy were dissolved into their atoms, being regarded as collections of individuals or abstract aggregates.

There are many variations and shades of this body of doctrine re-

---

[8] Translated by I. R. Mez. Eugene, Ore., 1931.

lated to the actual practice and policy of the period. It was not of course the only doctrine, but it was the ruling doctrine of the age. The doctrine itself has undergone a substantial transformation in its theoretical formulation. The classical school with its objective theory of value was succeeded by the psychological and mathematical school with its subjective theory of value and finally by the neoclassical school (Marshall), which combines the two versions, being really a transition between the third and fourth stage. But the main thread was maintained in these various schools—the commercial version of economics suited to the needs of the commercial society.

Neosocialism

The ruling doctrine of our age in European countries can, I think, best be described as socialism, and it exists in two basic versions; an Eastern, strongly orthodox, Marxian version for the forcible and energetic development of backward countries through very intensive capital expansion and stringent command of all resources; the other, the Western doctrine, for the full use of productive resources for the benefit of the community. The emphasis in the Eastern version is on capital development at the cost of standards of living to bridge the widening gap between low- and high-income countries; that in the Western version is on full employment and the raising of the standard of living.

The dilution of socialism into neosocialism is strictly related to the country's economic standard. Low-income countries have a very strong dose of socialism, high-income countries a very weak one. Accordingly, countries which now occupy a medium position between low- and high-income levels, such as Great Britain, have also a medium dilution of socialism. I would venture to describe socialism in the Western version, as seen for instance in

British contemporary trends of thought, as neosocialism, in the following summary portrait:

The central idea of the Western version is planning. A national economy must be subjected to planning, i.e., to an over-all control of national resources to be utilized as a whole and in the interest of the community.

The idea of planning is closely bound up, not only with the increasing moral and political cohesion of the nation in modern times, but also with changes in the structure of national economy, in technology, defense, and the pattern of international relations. The speed of technical progress, monopolization, and concentration, the ever growing field of scientific resources, political emergency, the demand for social security and full employment —all these forces contribute to the drive towards planning. The widening gap between potential and actual income which has been observed in the period between the two wars and the fear of its return in still more acute forms play a great part in the drive towards planning. The full utilization of the nation's resources is a main preoccupation, and since under a *laissez-faire* system full use of these resources is uncertain, this aim is one of the basic arguments for adopting the technique of planning.

The ambition of economists and statesmen is therefore to devise methods of planning with a minimum of controls and with minimum cost to the society as a whole, using especially controls designed to prevent the waste of national resources. Public advice, guidance, example, inducement, co-operation are preferred to compulsion and prohibition. The controls are brought into operation principally where an evident and appreciable gap occurs between social and private costs, between potential and actual income, between the national interest and private interest.

An attempt is made to bring the private interest more and more into harmony with the interest of the nation as a whole, and to think in terms of the whole, seeking to subordinate the parts to the requirements of the whole. Over-all agencies are established which are designed to view every economic issue in terms of the cost accruing to the community as a whole, that is, not in terms of financial expenditure (transfer expenditure), but in terms of real expenditure to the whole community, or in other words, in terms of employment, productivity, and welfare.

The fullest and best utilization of the national resources is the general criterion of all economic institutions and arrangements. The monetary system, the flow of savings and investment, the balance of trade, the distribution of income, the movement of prices and wages, the budget—all are subjected to the test of whether they help to achieve the fullest and best utilization of national resources. Responsibility for the fullest and best utilization of resources rests primarily with the public authorities, and the mechanism to insure it is called planning. Until full employment is reached, the first criterion is rise in employment; thereafter, rise in productivity. The best expression of this general test is found in the concept of national income in real terms, made up of goods and services, including public services. Everything is subjected to the general test: Does it help to increase the national income in terms of welfare, employment, and efficiency?

In this system the self-interest of the economic man is not glorified as in former times. It still has a useful function to perform, but as a motive it must be supplemented by a new motive, that of making the maximum contribution to the national income. A new form of competition which is now coming to the fore, group competition, as seen in savings campaigns or in wartime production drives, may be as powerful a stimulus towards improvement as was self-interest in the old pattern.

Accordingly, it is argued that industries are to be divided into three groups:

The first group of basic industries should be socialized, but only so far as the institution of national ownership in a given industry proves superior to that of private property.

The second group should be privately owned, but under control so far as controls are necessary for achieving nationally important objectives.

The third group of industries of minor importance may be left privately owned and altogether free.

All arrangements in this respect are a mere question of comparative advantage. The division into these three groups must be kept fluid, depending on changing conditions. The scope of socialization must be strictly related to the question of monopoly, capital investment, and higher productivity of both institutions, and the scope and the intensity of controls are strictly subordinate to the scope of national objectives.

But industry, although under private ownership, is not merely a private but a national asset, and should therefore be used for the common good, especially as regards its full utilization and highest productivity. The idea of planning requires a reformulation of property rights, a new ethos of ownership, and this is actually in process of formation. Private property is no longer the invulnerable sacred right of Roman law; it is becoming once more, as in medieval thought, *ius procurandi et dispensandi* (the right of getting and spending) instead of *ius utendi, fruendi, ac abutendi* (the right of using, enjoying, and abusing). New forms of amphibian property, property under public control, are coming into existence.

The concept of national income applied as a general test has the most revolutionary effects in relation to an economic approach. From it follows the idea of national waste, which embraces elements never hitherto regarded as waste, for instance, waste in population (through premature death or sickness), in undereducation, in undernourishment. It also leads to the distinction between income-creating and other expenditure. The expansion of public services, especially of social, educational, or research services, or of public investment, is in many cases equivalent to an expansion of national income. The line of demarcation between national expenditure in real terms and national income is dropped; they are only two sides of the same thing. More expenditure in real terms is equivalent to more income in real terms, and *vice versa*. All that matters is that the expenditure shall be of the right kind, namely that it shall help to achieve the maximum output of the community.

The limiting factors in achieving the maximum income are only national resources in size and pattern (composition in kind), capital and human resources as well as the balance of payment, i.e., resources which can be supplemented by way of export, credit, and investment from outside. Therefore first consideration must be paid to those resources which are at a minimum and to the removal of all the bottlenecks which are a hindrance to full employment and full productivity. The most important bottlenecks are of course those in the necessary imports, such as food and raw materials.

It is exactly at this point that socialism penetrates the field of international relations, demanding extension beyond the national state.

After Socialism—What?

Probably some of the noblest inspirations of mankind are centered around what is called socialism. But there is much wishful thinking in socialism which may bring about its downfall even more quickly than economic liberalism fell. Liberalism proved unworkable because it assumed as real what was only hypothetical. It believed in an economic man, in the inherent justice of free bargaining between capital and labor, in the automatic adjustment of economic forces.

The assumptions of socialism are also to a great extent hypothetical. The social man assumed by socialism does not yet exist in reality, any more than the economic man existed. The social man is a man moved by the national interest, who is willing to make sacrifices for the community in his work and leisure whenever the community shall ask for it. If less spending on consumers' goods is required, the social man will act accordingly, putting away greater savings. If greater productivity is required, he will work harder or longer. Socialism requires for its smooth working the real operation of a national-interest motive as a general incentive, besides the old incentives to a great extent replaced or diminished. The old incentives, based mostly on fear and want, above all on fear of unemployment, disappear in a fully employed welfare economy. And positive incentives (the carrot) are not always strong enough to replace the stick. The establishment of minimum wage rates, which become the rates of the trade, the tendency to peg wages and prices, together with excessive taxation, produce a certain sluggish atmosphere, especially in countries with a traditional psychology and a traditional standard of living.

The problem of economic incentives in a planned economy has assumed dimensions never dreamed of before. The liberal economist rarely investigated that problem, which was regarded as largely nonexistent. Of course a man had a strong incentive to "get on" in his work, because otherwise he would have to "get out," and outside the gates there were plenty of men waiting for his job. But as the "stick" is being removed and the "carrot" is being offered more and more liberally in social and welfare services, the problem of incentives comes to the forefront.

The educational work in bringing home to the worker the need for higher productivity and close co-operation with management, the institution of joint production councils and other forms of joint consultation, the change over to piecework, new ways of supervision and foremanship and new ways of discipline through workmen's representatives may bring a solution to the problem of incentives. But no one can contend that this problem has already been solved and that the socialist economy has resolved its contradiction, the contradiction of developing collective institutions under individual psychology. There is no doubt that a certain amount of altruism, i.e., the operation of national interest as an incentive, is needed to make free socialism work in practice.

Another big problem not yet solved is the status and rôle of the trade unions in a neosocialist economy. Their bargaining power is being enormously strengthened by full employment and by accession to power. Indeed under socialism they almost reach the highest peak in their power and status. But that raises great issues. Will this rise in status and power be accompanied by a sense of responsibility and self-discipline? And will the trade unions be able to sell their policy, if unpopular, to their members?

The problem is not so much whether trade unions will state the right policy, but whether they will be able to apply it against passive resistance from those on whom they depend for support. Unions are by their nature sectional organizations for protecting sectional interests of their members, who regard them as their representatives to do their bidding. The workers would like to retain the functions of the unions as "watchdogs" of their particular interests both in the offensive and defensive sphere. But the field of both offensive and defensive action in a socialist economy is narrowing, and the unions have to accept more and more responsibility for keeping industrial peace and discipline.

The problem arises, Can the sectional interests be turned into nationalist interests? or, to put the issue in a nutshell, Will trade unions abstain from pressing their claims for higher wages, shorter hours, or other benefits in working conditions, if these demands do not conform with the national interest?

Many writers have envisaged the necessity of the reform of the inner organization and structure of trade unions under the impact of planning and full employment. Unions would have to develop into unions of industrial discipline seeking a rise in productivity and efficiency. Their membership would mean something more than the payment of subscriptions and the duty to join in strikes; it would mean active co-operation in the task of establishing social democracy, in making free socialism work in practice. The assumption that the task of trade unions is to restrict hours of work, to raise wage-rates, to reduce the supply of manpower from outside, and to lower the effort of the worker would have to be replaced by the contrary principle that the unions must see that everyone does his bit to the full, making the greatest contribution towards the common product in accordance with the share he has a right to expect. The union would be a watchdog of the national interest as well as that of its own members.

It is a common experience of many democratic countries that planning in times of emergency is relatively easy and runs smoothly, while planning for prosperity in peacetime encounters extraordinary difficulties. The reason for this is that in any schemes of planning for prosperity there arise from the start so many claims and demands from various pressure groups for economic benefits and advantages, which, in the atmosphere of a drive for prosperity, are extremely hard to refuse. And those claims often end in wrecking the schemes.

There is another limitation of neosocialist planning, one residing in international relations. Full employment at fair wages means a substantial rise of propensity to import food, raw materials, and other necessities and comforts. The increased imports must be paid for by exports. But the capacity to export depends on the propensity of other nations to import. This in turn depends on full employment in other countries, practising a relatively free international trade. But what if that assumption too fails in practice?

Many writers have contended that socialism in one country is just a dream, that socialism needs for its full working a firmly established international framework. And we can now see in the light of experience how far they were right. Socialist planning needs a high degree of international unity in the supply of necessities of life, a federation or confederation of states with a concerted policy in regard to money, credit, investment, and employment. By a concerted policy we mean such a policy as will raise the propensity to import more or less in a harmonious measure.

Last but not least we come to another unresolved paradox which the new nationalized industries have revealed quite clearly, namely, to the human factor in industrial relations. Socialism was a protest, not only against the material exploitation of the worker, with his chronic anxiety of unemployment and destitution, but also against the disregard of human values in industrial production, against the subjection of man to the dictates of profits. The personality of the worker, his satisfaction, dignity, self-esteem, his mental and spiritual balance were often crushed by the impersonal industrial machine. But the first steps of socialist action prove that there is no remedy in this respect in the nationalized industries, where often strict bureaucratization takes on a specially discouraging aspect. Common experience seems to prove that nationalization makes little difference to the status of the worker, or to his contentment. The nationalized industries appear to be susceptible to grievances to no small extent.

There is a certain weakness in nationalized industries, in their tendency toward centralization and bureaucratization, which has not been checked and counteracted. Here again only experience can show whether those tendencies are inherent in the system or whether they can be removed by certain compensatory institutions.

But there is certain justification for the growing belief that the coming age will be the age of a psychological rather than a purely economic revolution, and that more and more emphasis will be laid upon the psychological aspect of human contentment and happiness. When the basic economic needs of families are being more and more satisfied, yet the people are frustrated and discontented, it is clear that something must be done in purely human terms to remedy the position. There is a definite need for "humanizing" industry, for more humanism and humaneness not only in public but also in private corporations, for permeating the whole industrial machine with an atmosphere of friendliness and ease, and for better understanding of the needs, desires, and aspirations of the larger masses.

Thus we see that full socialism is so far not a fact but an aspiration. Whether it can withstand the storms of our age has not yet been tested. There is a great deal of wishful thinking and illusion about its working, its possibilities and realities, which make the position still worse. Aspirations and desires, ideas and ideals are mistaken for realities, and the general assumption is made that it is enough to put the issues clearly before people in order to make them accept what is best for the common good. A new doctrine of social harmony is preached and developed, and the socialists forget that the theory of socialism grew up as the theory of conflicts. Life is harmony only on its highest plane; on its lower planes it is all conflict, with more conflicts within a conflict. It is really a tangle of conflicts; that is why it is so difficult to understand and handle. Therefore no logical system can do it justice. No "ism," even the most noble and the most realistic, can embrace the whole stream of life, which goes on breaking out in all directions, transforming, changing, and rising.

The "isms" can express the main aspirations of a given age, they can be its guiding light for a while, but they can hardly organize all the creative forces, which are far more than any "ism" can embrace.

IV

THE DOCTRINE OF PLANNING

Economic Study on Three Planes

Economic study can be conducted on three planes, or from three points of view:

1. That of an individual striving for wealth.

2. That of a group, such as a trust, ring, cartel, "community of interest," trade union, or other trade association, striving for wealth and security on behalf of the whole group.

3. That of society as a whole, as represented by the state, which has its own objectives, these being more and more oriented towards obtaining the highest real national income.

The three points of view cover more or less three sectors:

1. The competitive sector (or market system) based on the automatic working of the market. This sector also covers the imperfect competition of single firms, so long as they appear on the market as separate entities.

2. The sector of monopolistic formations or group activities represented by the network of monopolistic organizations which make their own long-term schemes, sometimes of a restrictive nature, sometimes of expansion and betterment, but always on behalf of sectional interests. This sector covers only group regulations

or group arrangements, and is not equivalent to monopoly as such (monopolistic positions). Alfred Marshall, who dealt with the theory of monopolies, explained[1] why he left out the group activities of trusts or "communities of interest," regarding them as a "superstructure" on the first sector. Monopoly can appear in all sectors.

3. Finally, the sector of planning represented by the general framework as expressed in the national objectives and the controls imposed to achieve those objectives.

There is no sharp line of division between the three sectors, which "shade into one another by continuous gradation," to use the phrase of Marshall, to whom economists are greatly indebted *inter alia* for his exposition of the working of "the great principle of Continuity" and gradation.[2] The three sectors do not work independently; one overlaps the other. They are three layers, the highest trying to overrule those below it, and all of them in conflict with one another. The sectors assume varying degrees of importance at different stages of historical development and in different countries.

In the first sector the main forces are competition, whether perfect or imperfect, and the individual's desire for wealth; and economic phenomena are studied under these basic assumptions. It is the field of competition between individuals, in which the chief actor is the individual.

In the second sector the main force is the search for wealth and security on the part of the whole group and through the group-action of sectional interests. Its main tendency is to counteract forces emanating from the first or third sector (that of competition and individual desire for wealth or of public controls) by activities

---

[1] In his preface to the eighth edition of his *Principles of Economics.*
[2] "The motto: *Natura non facit saltum* is specially appropriate to a volume on *Economic Foundation." Ibid.*

directed at strengthening or stabilizing the favorable positions of certain groups and safeguarding their long-term interests. It is the field of co-operation within the group and of rivalries among groups. Here the main actor is the group.

In the third sector the main driving force becomes more and more the maximization of national income, and its basic assumption is that there is some authority which has a controlling influence or power of advice and guidance over the whole field of national economy. It is the field of national solidarity in internal relations and of state rivalry in external relations. Here the main actor is the state, which seeks to overcome all hindrances emanating from the first and second sector.

The classical economists concentrated their study on the first sector, basing it on the assumption of competition and individual desire for wealth. As John Stuart Mill put it in his System of Logic:

"Political Economy concerns itself only with such social states as take place in consequence of the pursuit of wealth, except those which may be regarded as perpetually antagonising principles to the desire of wealth, namely aversion to labour, and desire of the present enjoyment of costly indulgences. Political Economy considers mankind as occupied solely in acquiring and consuming wealth; and aims at showing what is the course of action if mankind, living in a state of society, would be impelled, if that motive, except in the degree in which it is checked by the two perpetual counter-motives above adverted to, were absolute ruler of all their actions."

The theory of group rivalries for wealth and its most important chapter, the theory of class struggle, belong to economic study in the second sector. The individual's desire for wealth on the part of the whole group is tuned down by the collective desire for wealth, although the most powerful members of the group assume a leading part in defining the interests of the whole, shaping its policy according to their own individual interests. In any case, what is sought is not the optimum of particular individuals but the long-term optimum of the whole group.

Marx, for instance, who neglected the first sector, concentrated his whole interest in the field of group rivalries, regarding the whole economy as the manifestation of the class struggle. For him the capitalist or worker appeared on the market primarily as representatives of their respective classes, interested in exploitation or in repelling the bent to exploit. For Marx the institutional arrangements in a society were such that the capitalist and the worker had to assume this role of exploiter and object of exploitation, willy nilly, being entangled in the net of social economic institutions, which forced them to behave in a special way.

The classical school did not see the class relations as embodied in institutions; while the Marxian school did not see the individual relations; but both are important for the appraisal of the economic forces of any society. The socialist writers have done much to bring into relief the institutional arrangements responsible for group rivalries and class relations, for the collective behavior of social strata molded by law, custom, statutes, or tacit consensus into certain patterns intended to protect their own interest against the interests of other groups. But Adam Smith spoke about the tacit conspiracy of the employers against the workers, and we can read more about it in Rodbertus, Marx, or the Webbs.

The third sector was completely neglected both by the classical and socialist school. Marx analyzed the "laws of capitalistic production"; he refused to subject to scientific analysis something which does not exist and which has not developed its own laws. He regarded all investigations about a planned economy as premature and "unscientific" with good reason, but with the result that when his followers took over the government in Soviet Russia, they had little to rely upon either in methodology or in substance. They had to try to find their way through the darkness completely unprepared. "Trial and error" were proclaimed as the most competent teachers. We agree that they are great teachers, but everybody knows how expensive they are. In fact very little economic theory has been developed in Soviet Russia, and the planning sector still stands as the Cinderella of economic studies.

In the meantime the need for developing the study of this sector has greatly increased. We have today a number of planned economies, with different shades and gradations, and with a variety of structural arrangements, beginning with full private ownership of the means of production and ending with complete state ownership. Great Britain stands on one border of planning, forming a half-planned economy with yet a predominant private industry and full respect for the rights of private citizens; at the other extremity stands Soviet Russia, a fully planned economy where the contradiction between the interests of the individuals and that of society has been solved unilaterally by neglecting the rights of the individuals. In the middle we have a whole range of patterns of planning, starting with France in the West and Czechoslovakia and Poland in the East. Thus more than ever is a study needed which sets out deliberately to investigate systematically in their institutional setting the economic relations in the third sector.

What are the assumptions made here?

We assume firstly that the basic motive working in a planned economy is the maximization of real national income, i.e., that the community prefers a greater real income to a smaller.

Secondly, we assume the existence of such social controls as are necessary to ensure this maximum national income—whether these controls are advice, guidance, example, inducement, direct or indirect control. Thus we assume that the state has developed certain institutions for looking after maximum national income, either special economic boards, or socialized trusts, or public utilities, or treasury agencies, or any other agency which is concerned with devising means for maximization of national income in various fields as well as *in toto*.

Planning in the sense used in this study means that the managers of enterprises look for guidance in their major acts of policy, not to the shareholders (who are concerned with maximization of their profits), not to the representatives of cartels, combines, and trusts (who are concerned with the maximization of profits of the respective groups), but to the public corporations, public boards, or public trusts, which are concerned with the maximization of net output of the industries; and they, in turn, look for a guidance to the supreme planning authority concerned with the maximization of the output of the country as a whole.

Paraphrasing Mill's sentence already quoted (page 144), we might say that the theory of a planned economy concerns itself with such phenomena of the social state as take place in consequence of the pursuit of maximum national real income, except those principles which may be regarded as sometime antagonistic to the maximum national income, namely the desire of wealth on the part of individual and group interests. In order to make the study realistic we must investigate the full effects of the national interest against the background of the two other fields, the competitive segment and that of monopolistic formations, the motive of maximum national income struggling with the individuals' and groups' desires for wealth and hampered by them.

There are no compartments of economic life in which the motive of national interest does not operate, but some compartments are more imbued with that motive than are others. The compartments in which it operates with the greatest strength are what we call strategic factors of the economy: basic industries and public utilities, the field of investment in general, money and credit and foreign trade. The national interest may be regarded here as exercising the strongest influence. In explanation or prediction of real events, however, a correct allowance must be made for the degree of influence exercised by other motives.

The modern trend is to restrict the competitive sector, and to enlarge the two other sectors, the second sector being made subservient to a plan by means of public controls. The planned economy is characterized first of all by the development of the general social framework within which the two other sectors move. They are free to move in such directions as are consistent with the wider requirements of a plan, which is basically a plan for development and betterment; if not, they are overruled by the mechanism of the plan.

The first two sectors have been much studied and examined, the free market sector having been a subject of continuous study for some 170 years; the monopolistic area since Marx's time, and especially in more recent years. Much less is known about the third sector, which has become an object of study only in very recent times; we might say in the last decade.

The chief interest of economists has now shifted to this third sector, i.e., to the study of arrangements devised for the achievement of national objectives, primarily for maximization of real national income, because, whatever objectives are pursued, the maximum output, in general, helps to achieve them.

I do not say that the laws of competitive economy, as described by the classical economists, are invalidated or false in our present-day economy; I say only that their validity is restricted to one sector of national economy, which has become a relatively declining one. And the same is true of the laws of a monopolistic economy governed by the institutions of group rivalries and class struggle. The forces of the third sector, which have come to the fore at the present time, are complementary to the former ones, and they are operating in a rapidly developing field. Thus in the parallelogram of economic forces the latter will have to be accounted for at a rising index.

Let us assume for the sake of illustration that the ratio of the competitive sector in the British economy in the middle of the nineteenth century was 90 per cent of the total economy, i.e., that 90 per cent of total income was produced under competitive conditions, the remaining 10 per cent under monopoly regulation, while a planning machinery devised for maximum total income was hardly existent. The index of the first sector has dropped now considerably, while both other sectors have developed enormously, especially sector No. 3.

I must warn the reader that the sectors are not closed, concrete entities but must be conceived rather as abstractions, i.e., as abstract fields in which the forces described are in operation. In real life the competitive forces, the group monopolistic forces, and the forces of social control are constantly corrected by one another partly by conflict, partly by co-operation, or by the neutrality of one sector. Any real economic phenomenon is the outcome of the three sets of forces.

Structural Change and Survival

It is difficult to compare different economic structures in their working and to pass judgment on their relative efficiency. The term economic structure or system is a very complex one, combining elements of socio-economic organization, industrial technique, and economic motivation (the rules of conduct). Roughly speaking, the socio-economic organization of the medieval society was the manor, guilds, and corporations, guided by the traditional ideas of distributive justice, *iustum pretium* and *iustum salarium*; that of mercantilist times, the manufactures in their original meaning, the exclusive monopolistic companies, and the state regulations, guided by the idea of favorable balance of trade; that of the liberal epoch, free enterprise in a *laissez-faire* economy, which, however, later became more and more monopolistic; that of planned economy, the new amphibian forms of property centrally controlled by planning boards guided by the concept of maximization of national income rightly distributed.

The technique in all these stages was different. The hand-mill and the water-driven corn-mill was the technical instrument of the Middle Ages; and advance in the manual division of labor was made in the early manufactures under the mercantile system. The first Industrial Revolution was the starting-point of the liberal economy; and the second Industrial Revolution of our own age, with its immense scope for application of scientific research and with its new technique of central control, is the starting-point of the planned economy. Economic motivation in the medieval society was the traditional desire to cover the needs of the traditional standards of living of the different estates; in the mercantilist times, the quest for maximum power through national wealth appears in the forefront. The liberal economy was governed by the desire of abstract book profits; in a planned economy there appears a new motive beside the old ones, still undeveloped, that of the greatest contribution to national income.

The changes from one structure to another are not abrupt. It is difficult to say at one exact time in a given country one structure was replaced by another. The structural changes were effected by the accumulation of numerous small differences in the structural pattern, which after a certain time presented really a complete new picture. The most marked differences are to be seen rather in the economic thought, the forerunner and the best expression of the changes impending.

Can we say then that new structure is superior to the former, in terms of efficiency? In a certain sense, yes, but the source of superiority is to be found above all else in the technical progress which is the main driving factor of change. All the other factors, however, especially socio-economic organization, play their part also. All that we could say on the ground of historical experience is that if a country based on the medieval structure were competing or fighting with a mercantile country, it could not survive; and the wars of the eighteenth century provide many examples of the superiority of the mercantilist state of Prussia over her neighbors. In turn, the French Revolution, victorious over mercantile states, and the Pax Britannica were also proof that the liberal economy was for a time superior to that of the mercantile system.

In judging the relative efficiency of various systems we should in theory compare them at their best, in their most efficient pattern at the creative stage; but in real life the alternative is in reality not between systems at their best, but between a decadent, worn-out system and a new system in its creative stage. The medieval guild society in France or England in the fifteenth century, with its monopolistic practices and exclusive rights, was not so efficient as it had been at its height in the thirteenth century or thereabouts. The mercantile system, creative and dynamic in its best stage, was in Western Europe ossified and decadent in the eighteenth century, and had become an obstacle to progress and development. The liberal economy in the period between the two World Wars, with its high level of unemployment and its large quantity of unutilized equipment, with monopolistic practices on the part of both capital and labor and restrictive schemes of production, showed a high degree of national waste unknown in the nineteenth century.

The main problem which confronts the nations in our age is this: Is a planned economy more efficient than a liberal economy in its present shape? For this is the decisive point in the historical approach to the problem of national survival. Certainly in one regard society resembles an organism. The evolutionary mechanism, or the principle of selection, works also in the realm of societies, but in its own way.

A social pattern is developed by the interplay (1) between man and society, (2) between different types of society in the community of nations, and (3) between society and environmental conditions, while national selection takes place first of all in the struggle for survival in the society of nations as a whole. The evolutionary mechanism of societies works, not through the power of reproduction, but primarily through man's creative powers combined with the struggle for survival in the frame of international life. The selective advantage or disadvantage of any social pattern in the ensemble of international life determines the natural selection of economic organizations.

If we accept the argument that a planned economy is more efficient and productive than the present liberal-monopolistic economy from the point of view both of defense and of prosperity (national output), the death sentence would be passed on the latter, since a nation adhering to it would have a selective disadvantage in the interplay of international forces.

The superiority of the technique of planning over a liberal-monopolistic economy is in one respect undoubted. It can achieve full utilization of the national resources, including manpower, and this achievement means a higher national income. The question whether planning can achieve higher industrial productivity per head was until lately mostly answered in the negative. But in war planning in the United States and Great Britain and peacetime planning in some European countries after the war, we have seen some instances of a considerable rise of efficiency. We can now prove by analysis that planning does not necessarily mean a drop in efficiency. The value of initiative and enterprise is undoubtedly very great, but it can be increased by supplementing it with public initiative and enterprise, by the technique of mass investment and bulk purchases, by the pooling of scientific and technical knowledge, by the dovetailing of industries and the co-ordination of their efforts, and by the leadership, guidance, and advice of public authorities.

It would of course be wrong to believe that the technique of planning is all that matters; that to secure the effective working of the technique it is enough to find the right way of development and progress. If any one country could choose between planning and additional raw materials, or an additional stream of technical inventions and discoveries, or additional safeguards for internal stability and national security, or additional capital formation, or an additional rise in education and skill, or better commercial agreements and larger overseas markets, the answer might be in abeyance, and probably in the end the choice would fall on raw materials, capital, technique, and market.

The fact remains, however, that the technique of planning is more needed whenever the drawbacks of a national economy are greater, compared with those of another economy, so that an effort must be made to overcome them by conscious readjustment. The technique of planning is less needed in countries that have a great industrial superiority over low-income countries with an inadequate industrial efficiency. The technique of planning which serves the low-income classes handicapped in the conditions of *laissez-faire* in domestic economy serves also the low-income nations which are handicapped in the *laissez-faire* international system. The technique of planning is in reality only the completion of the modern industrial technique. It is involved in the second Industrial Revolution, just as was the *laissez-faire* system in the first Industrial Revolution.

The Organic and Moral Elements in the National Economy

The age of planning stresses the part played by the element of creation, i.e., of a new and purposeful shaping of national economy. But it would be wrong to regard national economy merely as "made," as something resembling a building, or, still worse, a machine. National economy is a living structure like man himself, because it is composed of living beings. There is no inconsistency between stressing the purposeful part in national economy introduced by planning and the organic part imposed by the texture of social life. We should never forget the two sides of social life which correspond to the two sides of man's personality. As Bergson[3] has put it: "The essence of man lies in his power of creation, both material and moral. Materially he is a maker of things; morally, a maker of himself. *Homo faber* is therefore our definition of man."

Man is created, but he is also made by himself; and the same statement applies to a society, which to a certain extent is a product of its own making, but is also the product of organic creation. National economy is something more than an aggregate of quantities of a number of institutions and activities packed together and surrounded by a customs boundary. Economy was rightly called "economic life," since its working and progress is really due to our labor and exertions and constitutes part of our life. Its progress is part of our own development as well as the result of change in our environment.

A human society is an organic unity, since it is composed of men, women, and children with their biological characteristics. It exhibits a living design, although this design changes with historic periods. It molds the individual born in the society or accepted into

---

[3] Henri Bergson, *La Pensée et le Mouvant.*

it according to a certain pattern. It is a functional unity, since its parts are adapted to the whole. The interdependence between the parts is not mechanical, but organic in the sense of mutual qualitative interplay, the changes in one sector being accompanied by simultaneous changes in other sectors. These changes are supported by one another and have a wide functional character—they are a correlated process with parallel phenomena.

When we study changes in the monetary and financial structure, or in foreign trade, or in the price and wage structure, or in industrial organization, the supervening changes are not the product of a single cause, but are the result of organic growth, mutation, and transformation.

National economy displays self-regulating and self-regenerating characteristics, a dynamic equilibrium tending to counteract any misdirection in the flow of human energy, unlike machines, which show a static self-repeating equilibrium. It adapts itself constantly to the environment, to the land, water, and natural resources, as well as to international life. It shows growth and evolution, being subjected to the test of survival and development in the great experiment of Nature.

In a way modern developments strengthen the organic elements in human society. The integration of a national economy is ever increasing. Many factors are responsible for this, some of them technical, some of them political and moral in character.

The enormous increase of means of communication in a wider sense, the lines of supply of power and light, banking, insurance, and service trades, all this gives impetus to the process of integration. Next comes the enormous growth of functional units of production, of large-scale factories and plants which bring together hundreds of thousands of men in their work, integrating them into larger structures. The enormous development of social control, of

155

control of the mind of the people by radio, books, newspapers, movies, phonographs, news services, is another very important factor of integration.

Political and psychological changes have also to be taken into account. Wars and emergencies bring the people of a country closer together, and the emergence of social and political man, who in part substitutes for the pleasure of exclusive possession of goods the pleasure of participation in national life, contributes also to the same development.

But human society contains not only mechanical and organic, it also contains moral, elements. It has always been known as a moral body. Its bases are social valuations, moral, aesthetic, and scientific, of fundamental importance in molding the socio-economic pattern and in the operation of natural selection in human societies. Since society is partly a product of deliberate creation, it is to the same extent a product of moral forces. These moral elements operate in the age of planning with an ever increasing vigor.

An organic body, a machine, a moral body, all these definitions of human society cover some of its aspects, being supplementary, not contradictory, to one another. All three aspects of human society should be kept in mind when dealing with social problems.

A scheme advocated by a planner will be an utter failure if it contradicts the organic or moral forces of a nation. The organization theoretically most efficient may, within a given environment and with the moral and mental characteristics of a given nation, prove an utter failure.

The Geographical Background of National Economy

Geographical factors have hitherto been regarded as economic data heaven-sent and unalterable. We have never thought of influencing them deliberately and taking them into account when drawing up a balance-sheet of gain and loss of our economic activities. But the universalistic approach to national economy imposed by the technique of national planning reminds us that economic activities must be judged, not only on their own merits, but also by their effects on the geographical background. The geography of a nation may be compared to the home of an individual. The home influences the individual's life and work, but at the same time his ways of living and working react on the home and alter its pattern.

The spatial control of investments plays an important part in planning, since long-term planning is conceived first of all as arrangement in space, distribution of an area into zones of investment. Planning has a strong geographical background. Space consciousness, particularly regional consciousness, is one of the outstanding features of our time. It is a paradoxical one. As space "shrinks," we are forced closer and closer into the melting-pot of world economy. But the more we are absorbed in this huge unit, the more anxious we are to retain our local individuality and personality. There is an apparent but not a real contradiction in these two outlooks, international and local. They are really supplementary to one another, and essential to the complete functioning of both international and local development. Each is a necessary check on the other.

Regional consciousness consists in the belief that people living in a certain area belong to that area and can, in and through it, contribute most to the community; that man's activities must be related to the special features of his environment; that every area, with its special climatic conditions, soils, vegetation, density of population, industries, and occupations, has its own individuality, which must be fostered and developed. The emergence of regional consciousness has been to a great extent strengthened by the lack of balance and the distress in special areas brought about by industrial concentration and overcrowding. And this new regional feel-

157

ing is helping to spread the idea of planning, from which regional reconstruction is expected.

Our geographical environment is constantly, though slowly, changing with us. We must see that it changes for the better. The changes can be controlled and mastered in order to bring about the pattern we desire so as to make an environment suitable for man to live and work in.

There are five kinds of geography which together make up our national background, and all are influenced in some measure by our activities.

1. *Physical geography.* On the surface this seems entirely independent of man. Yet it is in part a product of economic development. It is enough to recall here a few of the changes which may take place, *viz.,* the influence of deforestation, or soil exhaustion, or of great drainage works to overcome climatic disadvantages, changes in the distribution of type and composition of soil by cultivation, and changes in the deposits of fuels and minerals by mining and industry.

2. *Biological geography* (the distribution of plants and animals). This type is even more influenced by our economic activities, since changes in this field depend largely on the cultivation and breeding of plants and animals in agriculture, horticulture, fisheries, and hunting.

3. *Human geography* (the numbers, distribution, sex and age composition of a population, the skill, health and educational standard of a nation). This type is the outcome of a number of factors, among which our economic, political, and cultural activities play an important part. Wars, migration, and the distribution of income are among the chief factors. We have learned to influence human geography in many ways, and our economic activities are primarily judged by their influence on population.

4. *Political geography*. This type includes the boundaries, structure, and administrative divisions of the state and other public bodies. The fabric of our national economy is to a large extent influenced by the requirements of defense, and by the size of the economy. Economic activities, on the other hand, have a direct bearing upon political geography, and upon political power in the conduct of the national economy. We must always remember this influence and take it into account when drawing up a balance-sheet of gain and loss in our economic activities.

5. *Economic geography*. This type is determined by the network of roads, railways, canals, airfields, ports; the location pattern of industries; the pattern of the sizes of plants, factories, and farms; the location of towns and villages; and is primarily the outcome of investment and employment.

Together, these five geographies constitute the geographical ensemble in which a nation lives. They might be called the national home, and they show a close network of interrelated factors. They are the "ground plan" for the economic activities of a nation. The economic activities have hitherto been dealt with separately on their own merits, without taking into account their influence on the national background. Activities in agriculture and forestry took place without thought of their influence on physical, biological, human, or political geography. Industry was located without thought for the preservation of regional balance and without reference to defense requirements. Similarly, the pattern of the sizes of factories and plants took shape with respect only to the needs of the optimum size of single firms, and without regard to its influence on the welfare of the nation as a whole or on human geography. There was no relation between the distribution of income and health and nutrition standards.

The comprehensive geographical approach to the national

economy tends to assess human activities, not only on their own merits, but also in relation to their full influence upon the composite national geography: on its beauty, its harmony, its integrity, its comfort, and the security of all its inhabitants.

The preservation and development of the national background in this new approach are no longer side-issues, but basic considerations. On the other hand, extraordinary investments needed for full employment provide ample opportunities for the development of geographical background and regional reintegration. Since investments for ordinary consumers' goods are of less importance in saturated, well-equipped countries, we can attempt to turn our geographical background into the most useful regionally integrated and beautiful home. We can accumulate large reserves in long-range assets, such as human, political, physical, or biological geography.

Circular Movements

The idea of circular movements in national economy is an old one which first came from the field of biological science. The idea was given great prominence in physiocratic thought, namely, in the circulation of the *produit net* presented in the *tableau economique*. It shows how the *produit net* produced by farmers makes a full circle in the process of distribution between three classes, coming back to the same farmers, like movement of blood from and to the heart. The physiocrats hailed this idea as the greatest discovery of their age, comparing it with only two other "discoveries": those of money and printing.

In physiocratic thought there was another presentation of these circular movements in the writings of Dupont de Nemours (1739–1817), who says that "nothing stands alone and everything holds together" in the realm of wealth, population, and culture.[4]

Sismondi has suggested another circular movement between annual income and annual expenditure, being convinced that the national income of one year determines the national expenditure of the next year. The annual income is spent, and the expenditure should be always of such magnitude as to absorb the whole annual produce. Income flows in expenditure, and the latter flows again in income.

Marx saw circular movements in the process of circulation of commodities. His formulas C(ommodity)–M(oney)–C(ommodity), or M–C–M are circles; however, the last formula he conceived as a "spiral," since money is exchanged for commodities in order to get more money, from which arises a question of fundamental issue: from whence comes the increment of money? His formula of simple reproduction, where capital is simply reproduced by gross income, the rest of which is consumed, is another instance of a perfect circle between capital and income. The formula of extended reproduction (capital accumulation), however, is a "spiral" which produces "contradictions" in the process of "the capitalist production."

Another instance of a circular movement is labor power–income–labor power. Labor power produces income, which by way of consumption is again converted into labor power.

We see that the processes of income–expenditure, production–consumption, capital–income, labor power–income, commodity–money, investment–saving are circular movements of different duration intertwined and intermingled. The economic process is

---

[4] "From wealth springs culture; culture increases wealth; this growth of wealth increases population; the increase of population keeps up the value of wealth itself" (1771).

so complex just because of the main circular movements, which interpenetrate one another and which are in constant transformation. Some of them have a long duration, and some of them are nearly simultaneous. The circle of income and expenditure is in its individualistic aspect a succession, in its social aspect a simultaneous process; the circulation regarded from one side being income; from another, expenditure. From the point of view of national economy as a whole, income is equivalent to expenditure and expenditure to income. We cannot say that national income determines national expenditure or that national expenditure determines national income, because these are equivalent. We can say, however, that the expenditure of some people produces the income of other people.

The circular movement: production–consumption is in its individualistic aspect a succession, but in its social aspect a simultaneous process. There is very often a perfect simultaneity, as in the case of services. In one act goods are produced and consumed at the same time, e.g., health–educational or recreational services are consumed at the same moment that they are produced. They flow into income and expenditure at the same moment. We can count expenditure on health services as part of national income of the same period.

The circular movements can be divided into two classes: circles and ondules with changing amplitudes and mean values, or other closed figures, and here lies the distinction between statics and dynamics. A static process is a circle or other closed figure, whereas, for instance, business cycle fluctuations or secular movements present ondules with changing amplitudes along varying paths. Economic life is a tangle of simultaneous movements of all the bodies which form the national economy.

The study of circular movements is very much encouraged by the theory of national income, because the latter is really a theory of the process of utilization of wealth and labor conceived as a circle or spiral. The national income flowing from capital and labor services is again transformed into capital and labor. A part of national capital, namely, its annual value, is used up and replaced by consumption, and may be augmented by the increase of the population and its efficiency; this in turn may be increased by expenditure on education, training, or health services. The using of part of the national capital for the purpose of increasing efficiency and welfare does not mean the diminution of wealth, but the transformation of material agents into human agents of production.

The study of circular movements contains still many hidden treasures, and many of the obscurities which loom in economic life could be removed if substantial progress were made in this domain.

Qualitative Distinctions

Distinctions between goods and services, or between industries, made on the basis of their physical, technical, or welfare characteristics were always rejected by the liberal economists on the ground that ethical or technical judgments foreign to the economic domain are thus introduced. Increments in the production or consumption of goods harmful to efficiency, welfare, or employment, and therefore to real national income, were treated in exactly the same way as were goods that promoted all these factors, so long as they were money- (and profit-) making. An increment in the production (and consumption) of a useful drug worth, say, $300,000 may raise the national output by saving life and promoting health and efficiency; while an increment in the production (and consumption) of harmful drugs or spirits by the same amount may cause a loss of national output by causing accidents, loss of work, and loss of efficiency; yet such differing increments were treated in exactly the same way by economists, who replied to all objections: "In economics we are not concerned with the ethical aspects." To emphasize this neutral attitude, the term "utility" was replaced by *ophélimité,* which means, simply, preference in individual choice.

The liberal economists were primarily concerned with the volume of certain abstract aggregate quantities classed together under their monetary aspect, such as investment, saving, consumption, production, import or export, employment, and their marginal yields in utilities or profits; they paid no attention to changes in the composition of those quantities from the point of view of their technical and welfare characteristics.

In the age of planning these matters will play a much more important part than hitherto, because on them the public controls will be based. The choice between activities based on surplus in marginal utilities or profits will be corrected by the public choice, which will weigh the effects of those activities on efficiency, welfare, and employment. It may be admitted, however, that the selective principle will play a much greater part in low-income countries in more rigid schemes of planning in case of shortages than in high-income and well-equipped countries.

Investment of the same amount in luxury apartments, or in munition factories, or in communications and transport, or in electricity or gas might have the same marginal efficiency of capital and give the same yield in profits, while bringing about different results in national output owing to specific technical or welfare characteristics. The effect of these on employment, welfare, and efficiency both in the short and in the long run may be different, owing to the different industries involved, a consideration which has little to do with the marginal efficiency of capital.

The effects of increments of imports on real national income will depend on the physical characteristics of the goods imported more than on any other factor. These effects will be different according to what is imported, whether luxuries, comforts, necessities, tools and machines, or raw materials.

When studying the effects of the destruction of war on a national economy, it is not enough to say that 10 or 20 per cent of the national capital has been destroyed, and that therefore the country will be poorer and its productive capacity smaller. It makes a basic difference whether the destruction was of houses, or of factories and plants. Only in the second case would the productive capacity be greatly impaired. Again, we must study the destruction by industries, since the destruction of some industries may impair productive capacity more seriously than that of others, owing to their technical effects. The position would also be different if the destruction were concentrated on one industry, as contrasted with what it would be if it were more or less evenly distributed over all industries.

The theory of bottlenecks assumes great importance in a planned economy. A shortage of a small margin of tools and implements or of power may prove harmful to national output out of all proportion to the monetary value involved, as was seen in the fuel emergency of Great Britain in 1946–47.

A planning economist will make more use than his forerunners did of physical units, bushels, yards, pounds, ton-miles, hours of work, standards of efficiency, accident rate, labor turnover. He will seek as much as possible to remove the money veil from things, and he will supplement and check the monetary units by comparison with physical units. He will seek to avoid as much as possible aggregate abstract quantities deprived of their technical, physical, and welfare characteristics (such as consumers', or producers', or investment goods), and will group the goods according to the functions they perform in a national economy, as raw materials, tools, machines, semimanufactured goods, transport materials; or

165

necessities, comforts, luxuries; or again in more concrete terms as food, drink, clothing, fuel, housing, furniture, roads and railways, hospitals and schools, leisure goods, and so on.

Such studies as the Economics of Food, or the Economics of Housing, the Economics of Textiles, of Transport, of Electricity, of Mining, of Iron and Steel, and so on in which the technical and welfare and employment aspect is combined with the monetary aspect will be elaborated and developed more than before. The economist will work in close touch with the technician, the two consulting, correcting, and checking each other constantly.

A planning economist will be more than ever aware that the direction of the flow of money is not a substitute for physical planning, for the management and direction of physical resources by technical methods. Physical planning is as important as, if not more important than, planning in monetary terms. The limiting factors appear mostly at the physical or technical levels of economic activities. To allocate money funds or credits and to ensure the profitability of certain investments are measures very often not sufficient to bring about the investments in time, if the technical problems are not solved. The preparation of investment plans in advance, the training of skilled workers, the ordering of scarce machinery whose production requires a length of time, the provision of transport facilities, hitherto lacking, or the removal of other technical bottlenecks are very often more effective in bringing about the investment in view than financial measures are.

The liberal economist had a preference for monetary measures. If he was concerned about the improvement in agriculture, he tried to alleviate the burden of taxation and to insure a low rate of interest, good prices, and abundant markets, whereas in the same situation the planning economist will be concerned, apart from financial measures, with questions at the physical and technical level. He will deal with educational and research problems;

166

with the efficient utilization of land and the improvement of the land-tenure system; with the proper use of fertilizers, fungicides, insecticides, veterinary drugs; with the improvement of equipment and machinery, and the adoption of improved varieties of crops and strains of livestock; with the adaptation of crops to consumption needs; with the removal or alleviation of the physical and biological limitations, imposed by soil and climate, by irrigation works or drainage or erosion control; with the improvement of transport facilities or of sanitation and the health of farmers. The physical and technical side of agriculture was taken for granted by the liberal economist; whereas to the planning economist it becomes the most important part.

The Theory of Social Costs

The theory of social costs marks the difference between the new and the old economics. It serves as the foundation of the new economic theory. The modern economist thinks more and more in terms of social cost in the choice between different investments. He tries to grasp, through the intricate and complex values of financial cost (private cost), the magnitude of real cost incurred on the part of the society as a whole. Thus a social cost calculus similar to the cost calculus in a single firm has to provide the tools for the problem of social choice.

The science of social accounting is still in its infancy. Valuable contributions have been made to it by Marshall (theory of the representative firm), by Pigou (theory of external economies and diseconomies), by Wieser (theory of opportunity costs), and Lord Keynes (theory of user cost), but no technique has been devised for the measurements of social costs.

Generally speaking, we can define the social cost of any article as the expense of its production incurred on the part of the society as a whole, irrespective of who in the community has borne it. In order to know the answer to the question, what are the social costs, we must bear in mind what the cost would be if the community were a single firm which could dispose of its resources freely without any restrictions. If anyone in the community can produce an article cheaper, if not hindered by monopolies, restrictive rights, or ignorance, the social costs would be reduced to that level.

The best approach to the problem of social accounting is the opportunity cost principle, the opportunity cost of a given good or service being defined as the amount of goods which must be forgone by its not being applied to its best alternative use. The social costs of armaments are the consumers' goods and/or leisure, foreign assets, depreciation of capital equipment which must be forgone to produce them. The social cost of providing coal for war factories is the cold suffered by the consumers, the loss of labor efficiency caused thereby, and the loss of output in consumers' goods industries caused by the shortage of coal.

Therefore, wherever the community as a whole loses nothing by expenditure, no social cost is involved. Thus we have to distinguish sharply between income-producing and all other expenditure. Income-producing expenditure generally involves no cost to the community as a whole. Investment or consumption expenditure borne by the Treasury in order to employ idle resources which would otherwise remain unemployed is of a financial character, but does not entail social costs, if we make abstraction from the user cost of equipment.

Furthermore we have to distinguish between expenditure for using real goods and services and expenditure for compensation of rents, rights, and monopolies, which represents merely transfer payment. If we pay for goods and services, this means that they cannot be used for other purposes (i.e., at full employment we must forgo some other produce). On the other hand if we pay for rents, rights, and monopolies, we merely distribute transfer payments; we are not forgoing anything. The social cost of decongestion of roads or of clearance of slums does not include compensation for land values equivalent to the capitalized rents which will be shifted from one place to another. However, we must reckon with that part of the rent which will not be shifted elsewhere. The cost of a site on which it is intended to form a public park is not equivalent to the capitalized house rent, because the house rent will merely be shifted to another place in the city or its suburbs; it is equivalent to the value of the goods which could be produced alternatively on the land if it were put to its best use for the community as a whole, after deducting other costs of production; for instance, the rent of farm land. When considering the cost of using capital equipment, we have to reckon the user cost, i.e., the difference between the cost of using the equipment and the cost of its maintenance and depreciation.

If we have to do with a specific factor of production, i.e., with a very specialized factor which cannot be used alternatively in the realm of national economy, the social cost of its use becomes zero, for if it were not used in this special production it would be idle and useless. Applying the same principle to labor, we find that its social cost in the state of mass unemployment is nil, for if labor were not employed in this particular service the alternative would be merely to waste it.

Expenditure on full employment is a financial expenditure, but it involves no social cost; on the contrary it is an income-producing expenditure—i.e., a community pursuing a policy of full employment will be better off than one that does not. Expenditure for relief which raises the standards of consumption of the poor as long as there are idle resources in the community is a financial expenditure, because no social costs are involved. This sort of expenditure is really an income-producing expenditure, because

169

some people will be better off, while no one will be worse off, than before.

Thus it is clear that we have to distinguish sharply between the state of full employment and that of partial employment, a state of partial employment providing ample opportunities for conducting the battle against poverty without social costs. After full employment is reached, we have to reckon the social costs of fighting poverty in terms of goods and services which must be forgone by the community that uses resources for relief measures.

Any expenditure incurred for raising health and efficiency and improving the skill standards of the population must be treated as a social investment which will find expression in the rise of national income. The counterpart of investment in machines is investment in men; very often the latter brings greater and more durable yields in national income than investment in machines. Investment in machines is based on the expectation of profits. If a poor man has no resources to invest in himself, the only interested party is the community as a whole, which can expect an increase in national real income from its investment.

To sum up, we can say that no social costs are involved in fighting poverty, if, as a result of the measures involved, some will be better off, while no one in the community need be worse off. To find such measures is the highest prize any social student can attain, because these measures mean an increase in real national income.

The Institutional Approach

Planning stresses the institutional side of economic phenomena, since institutions are purposeful social arrangements, whether they are based on law, practice, organization, or policy. Planning means pursuing some objectives and calling into existence institutions which help to attain these objectives. The economy becomes purposeful and therefore more institutional. Social arrangements are made for most segments of national economy. Money and banking, saving and investment, foreign trade and internal trade, wages, profits and rents, prices and costs—all these are subjected to certain social arrangements, all have a certain institutional and organizational setting.

The institutional setting was of course always existent, although neglected by the classical school. In the age of planning the institutional setting becomes more striking and visible because it is subject to deliberate changes in relatively short periods.

The planning economist is an institutionalist and behaviorist. He studies mass behavior in order to control it with the least effort. Any excess of control above the necessary minimum is a waste of resources, and his success in effective control is first of all measured by its economy. This implies a thorough knowledge of mass behavior in its psychological and organizational setting.

The economist studies institutions in order to perfect them and make them subserve the objectives for which he plans. The most general criterion is the maximization of national income. This is the most general purpose for any economic institution. Money, foreign trade, wages, investment, or saving have to assure such an institutional setting as will enable the society to put all its productive forces to the fullest and best use.

When Marx stated that in the eternal clash between the "productive forces" (*Produktions Kräfte*) and the institutions (*Produktionsverhältnisse*), the productive forces are eventually always victorious, whereas the institutional obstacles to the full and best utilization of resources are always being removed, he expressed his optimism in the evolutional process and his belief in eternal progress. In a way a planning economist who serves the requirements of a planned economy can justify this optimism, because the basic orientation is to remove all institutional obstacles and thereby to free the productive forces of the community. The basic preoccupation of the planning economist is to make arrangements such that the clash between the productive forces and institutions is resolved as quickly as possible.

In studying institutions the planning economist is first of all confronted with the problem of interdependence of institutions, a problem very much neglected by the classical school. The classical economist treated institutions as quite independent variables. The question whether a gold standard is preferable to paper money, whether multilateral is better than bilateral trade, or whether free wages are superior to collective bargaining was posed in an abstract way, in isolation from its institutional setting, as if one institution could be severed from the whole set of institutions to which it belonged.

Actually, a single institution is not an individual item in an unorganized collection, but a part, strictly linked with the whole pattern of structural setting and subservient to it in its functions. There is no sense in asking the question whether the gold standard is preferable to a paper currency, since the gold standard can only work effectively in conjunction with other institutions such as free trade and free enterprise; where such institutions are lacking, the gold standard cannot work. Under a monopolistically or collectively controlled trade, the gold standard could not work. There is no sense in asking whether free wages are preferable to union wages, or collective bargaining to public arbitration, since the institution of free wages was strictly linked with other free institutions, i.e., with the working of certain motives and pattern of behavior which belong mostly to the past.

The study of interlinks and interactions between institutions is an exciting field of investigation which will carry the greatest weight in our dynamic age. We do not yet know really what are, in the long run, the interlinks between full employment and wage systems, or between a trade system and monetary institutions, or between a controlled wage system and private property.

We must investigate what is the substance and what are only the modes, i.e., what are the primary and necessary and what are the secondary and accidental features in any institution. What is essential in the discharge of the basic function of this institution, and what is accidental, which can be removed or altered? Sometimes what we regard as accidental occupies the most essential key position, and by removing it we endanger the future of the whole set of institutions.

Finally, we must study the secular trends of institutions in order to see in what direction they are moving. By demonstrating the trend of changes of an institution, we can figure out the direction in which it will move in the future. Thus the institutional side, so long neglected by the economists, comes to the fore in our study, and a closer link is established between economics and sociology and between economics and social pyschology.

Target and Balance Economy

There are two conceptions of a planned economy. One of them can be termed a balance economy, the other a target economy. The balance economy is aimed at stabilization of employment at a high level and the avoidance of booms and slumps. There are no other objectives apart from regularity of employment. The business cycle is carefully watched by an economic intelligence service, and wherever signs of slackening activity appear the planning authorities take early action to avoid unemployment. The authorities plan ahead in order to balance the failure in effective demand, either by extraordinary investment works or by release of extraordinary consumers' demand. The public authorities have to provide the balance between the value of national output at stabilized prices and the aggregate of the effective demand in such a way that the market can absorb the whole output produced by the whole working population. The national economy is more watched than regulated by the planning authorities, who intervene only in case of expected boom or slump.

The balance economy is subject to an "antibusiness cycle planning," and some economists are very keen in pointing out that it is an ideal solution because it combines the virtues of a liberal with that of a planning world. We must confess to not sharing the beliefs or rather illusions of this group of economists, for economic as well as for social psychological reasons. The achievement of full employment is a much easier task than the maintenance of full employment, which is a much bigger proposition, requiring a great many standing controls. Apart from that, the need for planning exceeds the objective of full employment, arising out of the whole pattern of modern life. Planning requires also a wholehearted co-operation on the part of the public, and no enthusiasm can be expected for the job of the economic intelligence service and for a formal unchanging objective fixed forever, such as full employment.

A very great drawback of this thermostatic planning, based on watching the status of employment, is the great time lag between investment decisions and employment. The time lag for the prewar German programs of investments was estimated to be between nine to eighteen months,[5] from the time funds were allotted to the time they were finally spent. Another estimate of time lag, made by Tinbergen for American experience during the depression,[6] asserts that between eight to sixteen months elapse between investment expenditure and the maximum employment due to it.

---

[5] See Leo Grebler, "Work Creation Policy in Germany," *Int. Lab Review,* March 1937.

[6] *Revue de l'Institut international de la statistique,* 1936, p. 173.

The total time lag between the allotment of investment funds and the peak employment resulting from it amounts in some cases to three years. We see how difficult it is to plan full employment thermostatically, even if investment decisions are made instantaneously, as the thermometer falls.

A target economy is a different type of a planned economy. It is an economy aimed at achievement of certain definite targets in national investments. The objective is not full employment as such; rather, full employment appears here as a necessary by-product of a national objective, whether this national objective is a war effort, reconstruction, development of depressed areas, a large housing program, development of transportation and shipping, development of agriculture or export trades, or, in backward countries, industrialization at large. The targets in national investments are planned ahead in such a volume that they are able to absorb the whole labor force. The measure of controls needed is related and subordinated to the objectives, i.e., they are imposed to such an extent as is necessary to carry out the program of investments. If, however, the targets cannot be achieved without an overstrain, i.e., when full employment is surpassed, the targets can be reduced. The targets change with time (three-, four-, five-year plans), with the position of the national economy, the needs and wants of the population being related first of all to the international situation.

A target economy provides a much sounder basis for a planned economy which must be centered in national objectives than does a balance economy. The national objectives can arouse enthusiasm and a spirit of service and sacrifice for the community which a balance economy cannot call forth. A balance economy is conceived as a static economy; a target economy is a dynamic economy on the march towards certain goals. A balance economy is conceived as an insurance economy; a target economy is conceived as development economy. A balance economy is conceived as an instrument for rescuing the citizen from the oppression and fear of unemployment; a target economy enlists him in a national service for objectives which transcend the field of his own interests.

The measure of controls in a target economy depends on the scope of the national objectives; if these are not excessive, but are modest and reasonable, the controls can be the same.

The Achievement and Maintenance of Full Employment

The problem of how to achieve full employment has been widely discussed, and there is a great deal of agreement about it among economists. There are many alternative methods to securing full employment by fiscal policies or by controls over private investment and saving; some of them have been investigated by Nicholas Kaldor in his Appendix to the Beveridge Report on Full Employment[7] or in the British White Paper on Employment.[8]

The common ground covered by all the alternative methods is the doctrine of effective demand. The flow of total outlay must remain high and stable. Such an increase in the total outlay of the community on home-produced goods and services must be secured as is sufficient to absorb the unemployed resources.

Fluctuations of private investment or consumption expenditure should be prevented by controls or inducements, and/or offset by public outlay on investment and consumption. The additional public spending is the greatest weapon in the armory of full employment. This may be regarded as the English-American doctrine of employment.

---

[7] "The Quantitative Aspects of Full Employment in Britain."
[8] See also the statement of the Australian Government, *Full Employment in Australia.*

There are certain tacit or explicit assumptions underlying this doctrine. One of them is that the additional spending will not be used to raise prices and wages. If it were, the task would be more difficult, and still more spending would be required.

Another assumption is that the capital equipment of the country is adequate to employ all hands in that country. If it were not, full industrial capacity might not go hand in hand with full employment. To achieve full employment for a country insufficiently equipped industrially is much more difficult, for it involves a much higher rate of investment, which is very often accompanied by a rise in marginal costs of production. For a country like prewar Poland, with overpopulation in the villages amounting to more than a fourth of the rural population, more spending is not enough to ensure full employment. Full employment in these countries could not be achieved by spending either on consumption or investment, but only by spending on investment at the cost of consumption standards. And even spending on investment must be safeguarded by the physical and technical possibilities of investment. If a country has no capital equipment for carrying out physical investments on a scale sufficient to employ the whole population, spending on investment cannot achieve full employment, unless more or less useless works are carried out.

The third assumption is that the pattern of additional spending will coincide with the pattern of idle capacity by industries, and that a state of over-employment in some industries will not occur before general full employment is reached. If full and over-employment occurs in some sectors before general full employment is reached, we have bottlenecks which hamper the achievement of general full employment. We may then have to reckon with a trend towards a sectional rise of prices and wages which by organic links with other sections may lead to a general rise of prices and wages. Sectional full employment within a condition of general underemployment is not a rare phenomenon, and it provides the most important correction to the theory of expenditure as the single key to full employment. The deficiency of effective demand must be offset industry by industry, which means that we must also take into account shifts in demand and the problems of technological unemployment.

The fourth assumption is that if the additional expenditure is used for additional imports, it will be possible to cover these imports by additional exports. If not, the whole program of full employment would break down owing to the bottleneck of restrictive foreign trade. Countries with large coefficients of imports, or debtor countries, are in a more difficult position in regard to the policy of full employment than are other countries.

The fifth assumption is that the additional expenditure will not be used to any great extent for paying off debts or for savings, but will be used for actual consumption and investments. If debts are paid off or savings made to a greater extent, this must be made good by additional spending on a still larger scale.

We see that the achievement of full employment is conditioned by this set of assumptions, and that public controls are needed to ensure that the reality conforms to the assumptions. The achievement of full employment presents a task of varying magnitude in different countries according to the relative amount of unemployment (open or disguised) and to the range of inequality in the distribution of income, on the one hand, and the capacity of capital equipment to absorb the whole reserve army of unemployed, on the other. Full employment in major industrial countries, such as Germany or the United States or Great Britain, has never been achieved in the last three decades in peacetime for a long stretch of time; and in wartime full employment is only apparent, since millions are serving in the armed forces and in civil defense.

But the task of achieving full employment is much easier than that of maintaining full employment once achieved. The achievement of full employment generates many forces which tend to overthrow it. The strongest among them is the rise of wages and prices. The workers have a better bargaining position and can ask for higher wages, and the entrepreneurs have a better market and can ask for higher prices. There is also pressure in the foreign exchange market leading to a worsening of the balance of trade. The increased volume of imports necessary to maintain full employment must be safeguarded by raising exports. Productivity standards in some industries where dissatisfying jobs prevail are adversely affected by full employment, i.e., by a seller's market for labor. Thus the whole economy is overloaded, and is far from being balanced. The whole economy shows signs of inflation, working under excessive strain and stress; and new controls are necessary to offset the effects of inflation.

We see then that whereas full employment can be achieved with relatively few controls, its maintenance is a much bigger task, requiring a much greater measure of control, especially price and wage control, and planning in general. Moreover, the longer full employment is in operation, the greater is the measure of planning necessary for its maintenance.

The achievement of full employment is one thing, the maintenance or rather perpetuation of full employment is another, altogether different, thing. The Keynesian school has done much in elucidating the problem of achieving full employment, but it has done very little in solving that of the maintenance of full employment.

THE ECONOMISTS FACING
THE FUTURE

Pocket, Head, and Heart

Some economic writers think with their pockets, i.e., they consciously defend certain interests although they are aware that those interests do not merit that defense. These are the small fry among economic writers, moved by fear, greed, or vanity, or simply by the necessities of life, and their performance is forgotten as soon as the ink has dried on their script. In every epoch we have a profusion of such writers, who are more or less insincere, but who find it convenient to move with the interest of the ruling class or clique against the exigencies of a broader stream of life or against what they themselves regard as just—I mean those writers who act against their own lights, disobeying their own inner selves, speaking only half the truth. In a way all writers know that they have but rarely the opportunity of speaking the whole truth and nothing but the truth, as they see it. After all, writers too have to pay tribute to the great force of social hypocrisy which operates in every society by observing the conventions of life and by respecting the rule of habits and of powerful interests which would otherwise crush them.

The distinction between the category of writers with which I am now dealing and all others is rather one of degree than of substance, but the distinction of degree is important enough to blot them out from the records of economic science on its highest plane. Certain other economic writers think only with their heads, using their brains to solve certain economic problems in an academic way, i.e., in a way logically or methodologically sound, but one not based upon their personal experience. They are often attracted to the most abstract problems, getting drowned in the deepest currents of methodology, classification, and verbal disputes about abstract notions and concepts deprived of practical or moral meaning. They are the intellectuals who very often excel in registering and filing facts, in sifting and classifying them, and in logical analysis. The "pure economists" belong to this category. They have contributed greatly to the advance of the science by their clearness, consistency, and intellectual power. They were the authors of systems neatly planned down to the last detail. But in spite, or perhaps because, of this, the systematizers were never among the great lights in the history of economic doctrines. They have not left a great imprint on economic history or the history of ideas. One of them was Rodbertus, whose socialism was of an intellectual or logical kind, and whose heart was unmoved by the suffering of the masses and their aspirations. Here belong too all the economists of the marginal or psychological school, whose analyses are often brilliant but make no distinctions in regard to economic programs or policy, being based entirely on hypothetical assumptions. In a way Nietzsche was right when he said: "I distrust all systematizers and avoid them. The will to a system shows lack of honesty." And what is more precious in a writer than honesty?

There are yet other economic writers who think only with their hearts. These are the cranks and quacks whose writing is full of wishful thinking. They have little sense of reality, being busy in building castles in the air, giving the rein to their fancy. They are the high-fliers and the enthusiasts, who lack the real stuff of visionaries and seers. Their imaginations are not tempered by a cool brain, sharp wit, and shrewdness of perception. To this category most Utopians belong. They are never among the stars of the first magnitude, although their imprint in history is sometimes even greater than that of the writers of the former category. Saint Simon, Fourier, Louis Blanc, Proudhon, Robert Owen may be named as belonging to this group.

Finally we come to the writers of the highest order, to the shining stars in the firmament of doctrines. These think with their heads, but the thoughts are accompanied by the beating of their hearts. Their ideas are rooted in the heart, but they come to full bloom only by virtue of head-work, by deep and hard pondering, reflection, and minute examination. The ideas of these writers are always personal, in the sense that they are based on the writers' own experience, which brings up forcefully one side of what life has taught them. Their ideas are the product not only of abstract speculation, but of meditation and contemplation as well, in which love and inspiration are involved. Their ideas have been experienced, not merely thought out. In a way they were fed by their heart's blood. Their ideas have become part of their being, as the armor and home of the spider is part of its being, woven from the sap of its own body. St. Thomas Aquinas, François Quesnay, Adam Smith, Malthus, Ricardo, Marx belong to this category. The difference between Marx and Rodbertus, between Adam Smith and Cantillon, is the essence of the distinction between the members of this category and others.

And here we can answer the question put forward many times by the present generation: Why do the economic writers of the present time, without any exception, seem to be second-rate, far removed from the first rank? The answer: Because they have excluded their hearts from the study of man. Economics after all is and will remain the study of man, and a study of man of vital importance, of great possibilities, and with a great future before it. No study of man can succeed unless the heart has a part in it. I hear the cry of the purists: "No heart should be allowed to enter the study of man; it will only obscure the basic facts, and befog the vital problems and issues." This is simply not true: quite the contrary. The heart gives us a deeper insight into the reality than the mere intellect can. The men with big hearts have always had the clearest heads, an unfailing sense of realities, and a sharp scalpel for analysis and examination. The heart provides only a pathfinder, a light or guide in the deep and complex regions where the best head without this guidance is lost. "To have a heart of fire and a brain of ice" is certainly a most exceptional gift, but it is truly necessary equipment for every great writer or researcher, and the economist is no exception to the rule.

Therefore my advice to my fellow economists, if I may proffer it unasked, is: "Do not be ashamed of the beating of your heart; not only are you allowed to use it, it is also your duty to do so. If your head is in harmony with the rhythm of your heart, then and only then, will you reach the highest regions reserved for the eagles."

Can We Reverse the Trends?

Economists can be divided into three classes. One group looks only at the present and sees only things as they are; to them the present reality alone counts, all else is utopianism. The "pure scientists" preserve their "pureness" by regarding and studying only what exists. To study the future is to indulge in prophecy; and no respectable scientist will do that, he leaves it to the quacks. This group keeps repeating: "This or that cannot be done, it would bring ruin to all concerned," and I have produced evidence enough of that attitude on the part of many prominent economic writers in the past and present. They are the conservatives, and to this category belong the greater number of the so-called "pure" theorists.

The second group looks constantly at the past, enchanted by old institutions, laws, and customs, thinking them "natural," "genuine," "organic," or God-sent. Institutions which endured for centuries or millennia are to be preferred to existing ones only recently established, because they are based on age-long experience. To this group only the past is real, and the sooner we return to it the better. No small number of economic historians belong to this category, which may be called "reactionary" in the literary sense.

The third group looks upon the future as the "real" reality. Reality is what may be called "becoming" (*werden*) not what exists now (*sein*). Change is the real essence of reality: everything is in flux and in constant motion. The substance of matter is itself nothing but motion. Thus we have to study the laws of motion of our institutions and structure. Since reality is motion, the study of the goals and targets of the motions is not prophecy, but a piece of scientific analysis, although it is sometimes clothed in a form of a forecast. The greatest economists, I think, belonged to this category. They were the reformers who showed the way to further development, and who by their work quickened that development.

In saying that future development can be foreseen "scientifically," i.e., by the system of exploration and verification open to all men versed in the study of the subject, do I mean that I believe in historic determinism? In a way yes, but only in a way. When I see a train leaving New York for Chicago, I know that with the greatest probability, perhaps 99.99 per cent, it will arrive at Chicago. I know that when a piece of work has been started in a factory it will be finished and will reach the market. I know that if a new invention has been introduced and proved a success, it will be improved and it will go on being improved. I know that if a road is being repaired, sooner or later it will be opened for the public use. In all these cases I can see the goal of certain movements, and I know that these movements will not cease until that goal is reached. Superior and external forces alone can prevent them from reaching their target.

Let us see what an economist can safely say about the future. He can safely foresee, for instance, that the future will bring more and better machines. Observance of the trend for two hundred years causes him to state that every year or every decade has brought more and better machines in industry, and there is no reason to suppose that this trend will come to a standstill in 1950 or 1960 unless some new force hitherto unsuspected comes into operation. The forecast of further mechanization is a safe forecast. Take another example: Observing the trend for the last hundred years, we can see that every decade has brought a constantly increasing share of the government and other public bodies in national income. This trend is manifest in all countries. It suffers small relapses over a couple of years or even over a decade, but on the whole it manifests itself as a strong and obvious tendency. We can foresee that this trend will not be reversed unless a new and unforeseen force suddenly comes into operation.

What of planning? Over fifty years at least we have seen the field of government interference widening, more and more controls being put into operation, and the area of economic freedom restricted. Technical, social, political, and security reasons are responsible for this trend, which is a deep and constant one. Looking backwards we see more and more controls added nearly every day. I have dealt with this problem elsewhere[1] and I need not dwell on it here. Can we really expect the reversal of this process,

---

[1] *The Planning of Free Societies.* London: Secker and Warburg, 1942. p. 267.

unless some great new force comes into operation which we cannot now foresee?

What of money? Looking back over three thousand years' development of the monetary system, we can see a constant trend towards the dematerialization of money. Simple commodities serving as money; standardized and later signed commodities; legal coin in copper, nickel, silver, and gold; then a gold-standard circulating in the form of a banknote, first convertible in specie, then in gold bullion; next a gold-exchange standard, a managed gold standard, using paper money and checks. The trend is unmistakable, and we can hardly expect its reversal, short of the appearance of some hitherto unforeseen force.

Or take the shortening of hours of work, which is of course closely connected with the process of continual mechanization. Can we expect a reversal of this trend, which has been operating for at least a hundred and twenty years? The antideterminists say: "If we wish, we can reverse this trend." I agree; the only objection I would raise is that we do *not* wish and will not wish sufficiently strongly and as a majority to reverse it. Our wishes and desires are part of the mechanism of this trend. And when we speak of "our" wishes and desires, we speak of those of the great masses of which we form part.

Our wishes and desires are perhaps the most important factors in the operation of any social-economic trend, but they form an integral part in its functioning. In certain circumstances, for instance in circumstances of cumulative and progressive mechanization and growing technicality of life and labor, the great masses of people have specific wishes and desires closely knit up with their whole pattern of life, and there are in fact no real alternatives to their wishes and desires. Of course, if any of us could impart new wishes and desires to them, we should then become a historical force of the first order. Did Marx, Engels, or Lasalle impart new wishes and desires to the great masses in Europe, or did they only express existing wishes and desires, organize them and give them new forms and a new life? The fact remains that these men moved in the direction of those trends, they followed the wishes and desires of the great masses. They did not reverse the trend of development; they only quickened it. If they had attempted to reverse these trends, they would probably have nullified their own influence and would have remained nonentities, in spite of the great force of their personality and expression.

Marx, who was a historical force of the first order in Eastern Europe, is a force of lesser order in Western Europe, and is of little significance in the United States. It is not Marx who made the revolution; the revolution made Marx. Men become great only if they can be woven into the whole pattern of life, if the current of life carries them onward, while they themselves do the utmost to co-operate with the movement by swimming with all their strength.

Great men are characterized, not by the fact that they bump their heads against the wall, but that they give vent to the wishes and desires of the people, quickening or lightening and ennobling the genuine trend of development, and, from available alternatives, choosing those which best suit their ideals and programs, while still moving with the stream of events. All of them move with the stream of events; the most powerful of men cannot change it. If they swim against the stream, they can hardly move; if with the stream, they move quickly; but they have an alternative, to swim across in a diagonal line, less quickly but at a good speed. The stream of events is the historical forces moved and molded by the Invisible Hand.

It is the noblest task of the economist to study the currents of life, not to see life, as most do, as a stagnant pool; to present alternatives to the public, pointing out those which are most consistent with the "good life" of a society as he sees it. But most economists of the present age are bumping their heads against the wall, with the result that their heads ache and their labors remain unproductive and are despised by the great masses of people.

What Can We Learn from the History of Economic Ideas?

First of all, humility. Economic truths are not invested with any hallmark of revelation or wisdom. We have seen how much bias and prejudice there were even in the greatest minds, even in those of the luminaries of our science, and we can reckon that there are at least as much prejudice and bias in every one of us today. Men always live under a thick fog created by the heat of their small interests, passions, and desires, and it is difficult for them to see clearly even a little way ahead.

We have recorded the slips and errors of even the greatest minds, how they failed in their diagnoses and predictions. How many more must be the slips of all of us today, who find ourselves in the heat of the greatest ideological battle which has been fought for many centuries. Probably all narrow-visioned specialists are wrong in their diagnoses, and still more in their predictions, because life is a totality and a complexity of factors, while the specialists know and tend to estimate factors of one order only.

Much of what the economists thought to be eternal is only transitory. Ideas are like plants; they grow and then soon wither away and most of them serve only as a fertilizing material for other plants. Thus the moral is: "You shouldn't be too cocksure about imposing your own ideas on others." Truth is relative to a certain range of assumptions, therefore to a certain stream of events and conditions of life. All doctrines contain a grain of truth which, under certain conditions of life, becomes the only valid truth. All doctrines are valid and true up to a point. This validity "up to a point" is the most common, but in fact the most important, truth in our lives! Everything is right up to a point, and from this point onwards everything is wrong. The doctrine of the medieval school, with its universal application to all mankind and its moderation as expressed in *iustum pretium* and *iustum salarium,* and with its emphasis on ethical discipline, is undoubtedly true "up to a point." The mercantilist doctrine with its emphasis on national interest and defense, on the balance of payments and balance of trade, is also right up to a point. So also is the *laissez-faire* school, with its emphasis on the benefits of individual competition and incentives, true up to a point. The socialist doctrine of purposeful co-operational planning for the good of society is also true up to a point, although at the present moment it seems more valid than any other single doctrine.

Democracy exalts freedom, but it often forgets about the delights of human fellowship, which can sweeten even the hardships and perils of war. The thrill of living in comradeship and fellowship with other men, the thrill of sacrifice, these have delights often not recognized by democracies, which put their whole emphasis on formal freedom. The neosocialistic ideas supply corrections to this system of formal freedom.

The right conduct of human affairs is difficult because we have no fixed, rigid principles to hold on to, but have to use our common sense in applying all these principles in the right proportion. Any, even the best principle, can go wrong if pursued to its bitter end. Hence the beneficial effect of tolerance. What you regard as wrong today may be regarded as right tomorrow; in fact it might *be* right, under changed conditions, and "change is the essence of life."

In the development of economic ideas we see certain patterns of change which make sense and have a certain meaning. We see great diversity, but it is diversity in unity. There are definite patterns of thought which are valid in a certain age and which can be covered by one of the great "isms," but even in that unity we see an enormous diversity corresponding to individual gifts, talents, interests, propensities, and different aspects of life. Unity should not be expressed rigidly as uniformity; it is only a thin (but strong) thread provided by the problems of time and the standards of culture, which permeate all representative doctrines of a given age.

The other thing history teaches us is that economic ideas are not an autonomous field of human endeavor, but are strictly related to the whole pattern of life. Economics is not the center of the solar system of man's thought; rather, it is a small planet revolving around a star of a much higher order.

The economic ideas of the Schoolmen or the economic ideas of mercantilism, or of liberalism, or of socialism were not conceived independently as a result of research in scientists' studies or libraries; they were closely woven into the warp of the whole texture of life, out of the outlook and social and moral values of their time. They supported the economic, political, and moral fabric of the community; they were part and parcel of the whole cycle of values; they were fed by those values, while, at the same time, they were feeding them from their own substance. It was giving and taking all the time. None of the great doctrines could survive as a whole if they were taken out of the whole context of their time, even as a fish could not live if taken out of the water. Each doctrine, like each institution, has a certain ecological environment in which it is rooted and into which it fits. We have not yet begun to understand the rôle of ecology in the breeding, development, and decay of certain ideas. There are flora of ideas which move and shift with time and place as much as real flora and fauna move and shift. Our own brains work in a certain framework, and are allowed to move within a given range of ideas by the whole pattern of life. Here we have the answer to the question why the same ideas are suddenly developed independently in distant places at the same time when the pattern of life demands their emergence. It looks as if we were all small cells in the same collective giant brain of civilized mankind.

But if economics is only a branch of a big tree, it follows that on purely economic grounds we can never go deep enough to uncover the roots of the problem. Economic analysis remains on the surface of any great problem of life and cannot bring us its real solution, because the roots are deeper, lying as they do on a different plane, religious, moral, social, and political. And we have to participate in life on real issues, not on the issues presented in economic analysis or academic speculations.

The issues presented in economic doctrines are very often blurred and fogged by irrelevant sidelines, and only after a long time can we see what they are all about. It is really difficult to penetrate into the substance of any great issue and to the core of reality. We are often misinformed about the real facts of life, and we are often out of touch with the most important issues of our time. There are primary issues solved on their own merits, and secondary and tertiary issues which are only solved on the merits of the issues to which they are related. We may call the first central issues; planetary issues are those which revolve around other issues like planets around the sun.

From clan to tribe, from tribe to city-state, from city-state to nation-state, empire, continent, and probably global organization— that has been and seems to be the main line of development. The medieval doctrine was related to a city-state, the mercantilist doctrine to a nation-state, the liberal doctrine to an empire-state advancing further; probably now we are in process of developing a new doctrine related to the requirements of a continental and even a global organization. I believe that doctrine which suits the requirements of a global organization will survive. The global organization is the primary thing, not the social or economic contents themselves. Not such and such a social or economic philosophy is the primary importance but the requirements of a global organization. I believe that the main issue of our time is to obviate national strife. The immense destructive forces revealed in the present epoch make international organization and human brotherhood necessary and imperative. No longer is pacifism mere talk and wishful thinking among a handful of friends. It has become the issue of our time, the "to be or not to be" of our civilization. Either men will succeed in bringing about a wider and broader allegiance to humanity at large or they will perish. It is no longer academic to talk about the decline and decay of our civilization; this decline is a real cosmic threat in which everything man stands for is involved. In what form, or in what way, an effective international organization will be brought about no one knows. But it will have to come. It is my belief that ultimately that doctrine will win which can bring about international understanding and human brotherhood. Thus every doctrine has to be scrutinized very closely not only on its own merit but also on its effect on the crucial issue: whether it will help or hinder in creating the stable and sound international framework which is necessary for the survival of man.

Economic and social issues are very important, but to our present generation they are merely sidetracks of secondary importance. They will once more become important when international organization becomes an actual fact; until that time they are merely satellites of the great, we might say cataclysmic, issue which demands, "unite or perish." We do not know whether international organization can come about without war, or whether it will follow the most destructive struggle that has ever threatened mankind, but there is no doubt that the supreme historic forces are definitely moving in one direction to achieve the protection of the human fabric of society from the blast of the great destructive forces of science. These destructive forces have not been revealed for nought; they have a definite task to fulfill—to compel men to live in a planetary political system revolving around a fixed center, so that peace and security can be kept.

In his *Leviathan*[2] Hobbes said: "During the time men live without a common Power to keep them all in awe, they are in that condition which is called Warre; and such a warre, as is of every man against man." Substitute in this sentence of Hobbes "states" for "men" and you have the position at our present day.

A new and greater horizon has been revealed before our very eyes. The defective and inert constructions built by national sovereignties will be destroyed and removed, and a new making and unmaking of states and empires will take place to accomplish the gigantic and crucial task for which our times so arduously labor. It is well for us to understand the message of our times, because only in that way can we escape bitter disappointments and avoid waste of energy. Only in that way shall we be able to build up a new stable framework for our civilization and culture.

Those doctrines, those movements, those states, those parties, those men who make the ideas of international and human brotherhood their own will win the day, while those who oppose this aim must decay and perish, unless we envisage a complete downfall of our civilization, a leap into chaos and barbarism.

It is remarkable that the two most recent economic doctrines—or really three out of four—paid homage to the ideals of international co-operation, but in practice none of them brought about this co-operation. Neither liberalism nor socialism today is very successful

---

[2] London, 1651, p. 62.

in promoting peace and international co-operation, and probably we shall have to witness new movements, with the sole emphasis on the paramount needs of our time. The economist can play a very useful part in serving those needs, because his whole training, both in the past and the present, has been permeated with the ideals of internationalism, a circumstance for which he was often reproached by leading industrialists and statesmen.

INDEX

INDEX

INDEX